# The Language of Drama

'Working through a remarkably rich array of examples, Keith Sanger reveals the key mechanisms of drama and shows how they contribute to such aspects as realism, characterisation, plot and performance. The terms and concepts are clearly explained and relevant. . . . Moreover, the activities and exercises really do work!'

Jonathan Culpeper, *Lancaster University*

This accessible satellite textbook in the Routledge INTERTEXT series is unique in offering students hands-on practical experience of textual analysis focused on drama. Written in a clear, user-friendly style by a practising teacher, it combines practical activities with texts, followed by commentaries and suggestions for further activities. It can be used individually or in conjunction with the series core textbook, *Working with Texts: A core book for language analysis*.

Aimed at A-Level and beginning undergraduate students, *The Language of Drama*:

- ◎ examines a wide range of drama scripts, including plays, soap operas and screenplays: from Shakespeare to Stoppard; *Coronation Street* to *The Archers*; *Sense and Sensibility* to *Sour Sweet*
- ◎ is illustrated throughout with specially commissioned artwork by the *Viz* cartoonist John Fardell
- ◎ discusses key aspects of dramatic language, including: conversation, dialect, narrative structure, cohesion, repetition and imagery
- ◎ explores contemporary linguistic research and applies this to the texts in an accessible way
- ◎ provides a comprehensive glossary of terms, an index of texts and writers, and suggestions for further reading.

**Keith Sanger** is Lecturer in English and Drama at New College (VI Form), Pontefract, and a team leader for AQA A-Level English Language.

# The Intertext series

◎ Why does the phrase 'spinning a yarn' refer both to using language and making cloth?

◎ What might a piece of literary writing have in common with an advert or a note from the milkman?

◎ What aspects of language are important to understand when analysing texts?

The Routledge INTERTEXT series will develop readers' understanding of how texts work. It does this by showing some of the designs and patterns in the language from which they are made, by placing texts within the contexts in which they occur, and by exploring relationships between them.

The series consists of a foundation text, *Working with Texts: A core book for language analysis*, which looks at language aspects essential for the analysis of texts, and a range of satellite texts. These apply aspects of language to a particular topic area in more detail. They complement the core text and can also be used alone, providing the user has the foundation skills furnished by the core text.

**Benefits of using this series:**

◎ **Unique** – written by a team of respected teachers and practitioners whose ideas and activities have also been trialled independently

◎ **Multi-disciplinary** – provides a foundation for the analysis of texts, supporting students who want to achieve a detailed focus on language

◎ **Accessible** – no previous knowledge of language analysis is assumed, just an interest in language use

◎ **Comprehensive** – wide coverage of different genres: literary texts, notes, memos, signs, advertisements, leaflets, speeches, conversation

◎ **Student-friendly** – contains suggestions for further reading; activities relating to texts studied; commentaries after activities; key terms highlighted and an index of terms

## The series editors:

**Ronald Carter** is Professor of Modern English Language in the Department of English Studies at the University of Nottingham and is the editor of the Routledge INTERFACE series in Language and Literary Studies. He is also co-author of *The Routledge History of Literature in English*. From 1989 to 1992 he was seconded as National Director for the Language in the National Curriculum (LINC) project, directing a £21.4 million in-service teacher education programme.

**Angela Goddard** is Senior Lecturer in Language at the Centre for Human Communication, Manchester Metropolitan University, and was Chief Moderator for the project element of English Language A-Level for the Northern Examination and Assessment Board (NEAB) from 1983 to 1995. Her publications include *The Language Awareness Project: Language and Gender*, vols I and II, 1988, and *Researching Language*, 1993 (Framework Press).

## Core textbook:

*Working with Texts: A core book for language analysis*
Ronald Carter, Angela Goddard, Danuta Reah, Keith Sanger, Maggie Bowring

## Satellite titles:

*The Language of Sport*
Adrian Beard

*The Language of Politics*
Adrian Beard

*The Language of Advertising: Written texts*
Angela Goddard

*Language and Gender*
Angela Goddard and
Lindsey Meân Patterson

*The Language of Magazines*
Linda McLoughlin

*The Language of Poetry*
John McRae

*The Language of Newspapers*
Danuta Reah

*The Language of Humour*
Alison Ross

*The Language of Fiction*
Keith Sanger

*The Language of ICT: Information and Communication Technology*
Tim Shortis

### Related titles:

INTERFACE series:

*Variety in Written English*
Tony Bex

*Language, Literature and Critical Practice*
David Birch

*A Linguistic History of English Poetry*
Richard Bradford

*The Language of Jokes*
Delia Chiaro

# The Language of Drama

• Keith Sanger

London and New York

First published 2001
by Routledge
11 New Fetter Lane, London EC4P 4EE

Simultaneously published in the USA and
Canada
by Routledge
29 West 35th Street, New York, NY 10001

*Routledge is an imprint of the Taylor & Francis
Group*

© 2001 Keith Sanger

The right of Keith Sanger to be identified as the
Author of this Work has been asserted by him
in accordance with the Copyright, Designs and
Patents Act 1988

Typeset in Stone Sans/Stone Serif by
Keystroke, Jacaranda Lodge, Wolverhampton
Printed and bound in Great Britain by
St Edmundsbury Press, Bury St Edmunds,
Suffolk

*British Library Cataloguing in Publication Data*

A catalogue record for this book is available
from the British Library

*Library of Congress Cataloging in Publication
Data*
Sanger, Keith, 1948–
  The language of drama / Keith Sanger.
    p.  cm. – (Intertext)
  Includes bibliographical references and
  indexes.
  ISBN 0–415–21423–8
  1.  Drama–History and criticism–Theory,
  etc.  I. Title.  II. Intertext (London,
  England)

PN1631. S26 2000
809.2–dc21                    00–032307

ISBN 0–415–21423–8

To the memory of my mother and father

Crispin and Natasha Critic are taking a brief sabbatical from the pages of Viz Comic to grace us with their enlightening presence. They appear courtesy of **John Fardell**.

# contents

## Unit six: The grammar of sound

69

Rhythm and stress 70

## Unit seven: Book to film

81

What? No narrator? 85

# acknowledgements

I'd like to thank Ron Carter for his continued support. Also Girton College, Cambridge, The Music and Drama Library, Wakefield and The Coffee Republic in Leeds' Waterstone's for offering refuge, a place to think and good books. Last, but not least, I'm very grateful to John Fardell for agreeing to pen some cartoons of his wonderful creations Crispin and Natasha Critic to head up each unit in this book.

The following texts have been reprinted by courtesy of their copyright holders:

Comic strip illustrations © John Fardell 1999; extract from *Accidental Death of an Anarchist* by Dario Fo reprinted by permission of Methuen Publishing Ltd and Einaudi Editore; extract from *Action* by Sam Shepard reprinted by permission of Faber & Faber Ltd and Bantam Books, a division of Random House Inc.; extract from *Alfie* by Bill Naughton reprinted by permission of Casarotto Ramsay & Associates Ltd (all rights whatsoever in this play are strictly reserved and application for performance etc. must be made before rehearsal to Casarotto Ramsey & Associates Ltd, National House, 60–66 Wardour Street, London W1V 4ND: no performance may be given unless a licence has been obtained); extract from *Angel City* by Sam Shepard reprinted by permission of MacNaughton Lord Representation Ltd; extracts from BBC Radio's *The Archers* reprinted by permission of the BBC; extracts from *Casino* and *Goodfellas* by Nicholas Pileggi and Martin Scorsese reprinted by permission of Faber & Faber Ltd; extracts from *Coronation Street* reprinted by permission of Peter Whalley and Granada Television; two extracts from *Dancing at Lughnasa* © Brian Friel 1990, reprinted with the permission of Gillon Aitken Associates Ltd; extract from *Death of a Salesman* © 1948, 1949, 1951, 1952 by Arthur Miller, renewed 1975, 1976, 1979, 1980, and reproduced by permission of the author c/o Rogers, Coleridge & White Ltd, 20 Powis Mews, London W11 1JN in association with International Creative Management Inc., 40 West 57th Street, New York, NY 10019, USA; extract from *Fen* by Caryl Churchill reprinted by permission of Casarotto Ramsay & Associates Ltd and Methuen Publishing Ltd; extract from *Lettice and Lovage* by Peter Shaffer reprinted by permission of MacNaughton Lord Representation Ltd; extract from *The Real Inspector Hound* by Tom Stoppard reprinted by permission of Grove/Atlantic Inc.

and Faber & Faber Ltd; extract from *Road* by Jim Cartwright reprinted by permission of Methuen Publishing Ltd (all rights whatsoever in this play are strictly reserved and application for performance etc. must be made before rehearsal to Casarotto); extract from *Roots* by Arnold Wesker reprinted by permission of the author and Penguin Books Ltd; extract from *Saved* by Edward Bond reprinted by permission of Methuen Publishing Ltd; extract from Emma Thompson's *Sense and Sensibility: Diaries and Screenplay* reproduced by permission of the author and Peters Fraser & Dunlop Group Ltd; extract from Ian McEwan's *Sour Sweet* © First Film Company Ltd, 1988, reproduced by permission of the author c/o Rogers, Coleridge & White Ltd, 20 Powis Mews, London W11 1JN and by Faber & Faber Ltd; extract from Timothy Mo's *Sour Sweet* reprinted by permission of the author and Methuen Publishing Ltd; extract from *Talking Heads* reprinted by permission of PFD on behalf of Alan Bennett © Alan Bennett; extract from *Taxi Driver* by Paul Schrader reprinted by permission of Faber & Faber Ltd; excerpts from *Twelfth Night, Romeo and Juliet, Macbeth, Othello, Hamlet, The Tempest* from G. Blackmore Evans (ed.) *The Riverside Shakespeare*, copyright © 1974 by Houghton Mifflin Company and used with permission; extract from *A View from the Bridge* © 1955, 1957 by Arthur Miller, reproduced by permission of the author c/o Rogers, Coleridge & White Ltd, 20 Powis Mews, London W11 1JN in association with International Creative Management Inc., 40 West 57th Street, New York, NY 10019, USA; extracts from *Waiting for Godot* by Samuel Beckett © 1954 by Samuel Beckett, renewed copyright © 1982 by Samuel Beckett and used by permission of Grove/Atlantic Inc. and Faber & Faber Ltd.

# introduction

Two things need to be said at the outset. First, a drama text is not the same as a novel or a poem. And stage drama is different from radio drama which is different from television drama which is different from film. Although we have the printed text, in one sense it only becomes realised in performance, in front of an audience. It is also not definitive; in most cases the text is 're-written' with each performance or direction.

This book examines the text on the page rather than text as performance. As you explore the various examples and forms of drama text think about the role of the actor, the effect that different actors might have on the language. For example, imagine and contrast Mel Gibson with Kenneth Branagh delivering Hamlet's lines, or Hugh Grant v. Brad Pitt as Willy Loman in Arthur Miller's *Death of a Salesman*, or Cher v. Emma Thompson as Elinor in the Ang Lee film version of Jane Austen's *Sense and Sensibility*. Different actors, different directors will re-define the language of the dramatist but, interesting and important to the realisation of the drama as these considerations are, this book is concerned with the linguistics of drama and focuses on the text as written on the page. The examples from stage drama and film take the script or screenplay as the written starting point for the actor. The examples from television and radio are actual transcriptions of the transmitted programme and considerations of re-writing or re-defining the text do not apply.

The second point that needs to be made is that dramatic speech is different from spontaneous unscripted speech. Consider the following example of actual talk. Try reading it out loud. It is presented following the conventions of transcription: (.) indicates a pause of $\frac{1}{2}$ second, and the square bracket an overlap/interruption. The dialogue takes place in a hairdresser's salon: H = hairdresser; C = client.

C: oh dear oh
H: so how are you
C: oh I'm fine (.) how's you
H: I'm alright yes (.) I'm fine
C: how's all the preparations for the wedding ⌈going
H: ⌊well I haven't really
done anything

C: (laughter)

H: for a while actually you know probably nothing more happened since I'd seen you last (.) I think I did most things and then stopped for a bit you know

C: but you're all booked up and everything ⌈aren't you

H: ⌊ah yes everything's booked it's just things like cars (.) we haven't got a car sorted

(Extract courtesy of Nayeema Chowdhury, Gosforth High School, Newcastle Upon Tyne)

This text was never intended for the page, so the real cohesion and fluency of the original dialogue does not come across: it looks messy, with speakers overlapping each other, and some parts are unclear – for example, why the client opens by saying 'oh dear oh'. In the real situation, non-verbal behaviour would have helped clarify what this speaker intended.

Attempting to re-create this on stage verbatim would cause problems for both actors and audience. For example, the actors would struggle to deliver the overlaps, and the audience would struggle to hear and understand. What this means is that drama scripts have to be very simplified in order to work: they may appear like real speech, but they are in fact something very different. At the same time, real dialogue is hardly ever staged for people other than the participants. As long as those engaged in the real dialogue understand it, it has fulfilled its function.

When you come to read extracts from modern dramatists and soap writers who get closer than earlier writers to real dialogues, there are still significant contrasts with unscripted conversations. Dramatic dialogue rarely contains false starts, hesitations, overlaps, fillers. The sense of the conversation would be difficult to follow and it would be difficult to hear each actor if there were constant bids to enter the conversation from the other participants. So even though the dialogue may appear to be realistic to an audience in the theatre, or at home in front of the TV, it never really is.

As a way in to the essential differences between real dialogue and play dialogue, tape and transcribe conversation at work. You might try family members at breakfast or at dinner, or friends in the pub. Ask for their permission to do this first, however. Having done this, compare your transcripts with appropriate extracts from soaps such as *EastEnders*, *Coronation Street* or *Neighbours*. If time is short, you could use some of the extracts in this book.

# Are you sitting comfortably?

## What is drama(?)

It may seem strange in a book on the language of drama to ask the question: just what is drama? But the word drama is used widely and loosely. It's used widely in the media to describe anything that seems to be unusual or to involve conflict of some sort. References to drama occur in the world of sport, moments of life and death, events in politics. Often the word is used to heighten the importance of events or their outcome. Examples might be: 'there was real drama in the World Cup here tonight . . .', or 'in a day of high drama, Tony Blair said . . .'.

Terms from the sphere of drama are also used to give events a label with which we can associate. So we hear, and read, of events which are 'pure farce', or 'tragic', 'scenes of carnage', even a 'comedy of errors'.

And when Karl Marx wanted to explain his theory of the cyclical nature of events he, too, drew on dramatic terms, writing that history repeats itself, first as tragedy, then as farce. For many people, though, drama will mean something make-believe which you pay to see taking place on a stage. And, for the most part, we ignore the artificiality of the occasion and surroundings, choose to forget that we are watching actors – that is, we 'suspend our disbelief' – and believe that what we are watching is real.

As far as the events of the drama are concerned, we may expect to see something happening, a change, an outcome, an issue explored, a character develop. We may be entertained, we may be educated, we may experience the Aristotelian concept of **catharsis**, whereby our strong emotions are purged away by seeing their representation on stage.

Take a moment to consider your experience of drama. Which plays can you recall? What makes some plays seem more dramatic than others? When Samuel Beckett's *Waiting for Godot* (1952) first appeared on stage it bemused audiences. In the first act of this play two tramps spend time waiting for someone called Godot to arrive; eventually a boy comes and says Mr Godot can't come today but will surely come tomorrow. In the second act the two tramps wait again until, at the end, the boy returns and gives the same message. This prompted the comment from a theatre critic that this is a play in which 'nothing happens twice'.

What, then, is the minimum requirement for drama? The theatre practitioner Lope de Vega stated that 'drama is two human beings, a passion and a platform' (Boal 1955). For him, drama studies the inter-relations of people living in society, rather than contemplating individuals in isolation. Drama denotes conflict, contradiction, confrontation, defiance. Later you can consider the form of the monologue – which, strictly speaking, de Vega would not class as drama – but, first, let us turn to the question of the platform, the space where drama takes place.

## The place

The space may well affect what kind of drama is taking place. Augusto Boal's Forum Theatre, for example, in which the audience not only comments on the action, but intervenes directly by coming on stage and taking over characters' parts, obviously works better in an open place with little division between actor and audience. Similarly, the

German playwright Bertolt Brecht chose to take his early plays which had strong political messages to his audiences wherever they might be: the factory, the canteen. The Italian playwright Dario Fo did the same with his plays which dealt with state corruption. Plays have been written with specific spaces in mind. For example, Jim Cartwright's *Road* (1986), which centres around several families living in the same street, is designed to be performed promenade style, that is the audience actually gets up and follows the action around. However, in all cases, separation remains a feature: a space (or spaces) for the actors and another space for the audience, whether these spaces are fixed or movable.

The larger environment – and its audience – can also affect how a play is received. Beckett's *Waiting for Godot*, which puzzled its first audiences, struck deep chords when performed in San Quentin jail. And, later, its message of survival made a similar deep impact when staged in a besieged, war-torn Sarajevo. Similarly, a play by Brecht with the message that being good means you are left open to exploitation by others, and ultimately abandoned, will have different resonances when performed on Broadway or in a theatre in provincial Leeds or in the Soweto township of South Africa.

## The set

Some playwrights give very clear instructions for the set and even for the characters. This forms part of the context in which the play operates. Plays are meant to be seen and heard but indications given for the set and the characters form part of the language of drama – albeit always in a written form. This, for directors and actors, is often their first introduction to the text.

Audiences rarely go into a play cold. Often, even if they don't already know the play, they will have some idea of what the play's about and what to expect from the publicity and promotion. Once inside the auditorium, the stage setting will also give some indication of the nature of the play.

Students of drama in text form are expected to do a bit of both: they are expected to read the descriptions of setting, but at the same time visualise what it might look like on stage. Alternatively, they can go and see a performance of the play, which will show them how one director and cast have interpreted what the playwright has suggested.

## *Activity*

Read the set descriptions given for the following four plays. What impressions does the language convey?

## Text: Set directions

1  The stage represents a comfortless flat in Manchester and the street outside.

2  A country road. A tree. Evening.

3  SIDNEY and JANE HOPCROFT's kitchen of their small suburban house. Last Christmas. Although on a modest scale, it is a model kitchen. Whilst not containing all the gadgetry, it does have an automatic washing machine, a fridge, an electric cooker and a gleaming sink unit. All these are contained or surrounded by smart formica-topped working surfaces with the usual drawers and cupboards. The room also contains a small table, also formica-topped, and matching chairs.

4  A melody is heard, played upon a flute. It is small and fine, telling of grass and trees and the horizon. The curtain rises. Before us is the SALESMAN's house. We are aware of towering, angular shapes behind it, surrounding it on all sides. Only the blue light of the sky falls upon the house and forestage; the surrounding area shows an angry glow of orange. As more light appears, we see a solid vault of apartment houses around the small, fragile-seeming home. An air of the dream clings to the place, a dream rising out of reality.

## *Commentary*

The first description, from Shelagh Delaney's *A Taste of Honey* (1958), is very brief; it paints a bare and bleak picture suggesting a play to match. It is rooted in a place – Manchester – and there is no suggestion of fantasy to hide what seems to be a setting of grim reality.

The setting of the next play, from Beckett's *Waiting for Godot*, is also brief. This time, however, there is a timeless quality about the description. It could be anywhere and any time; the here and now is apparently not important and this might suggest a play concerned with timeless, universal ideas.

The third description is quite different. This is a specific and individualised location: the Hopcroft's kitchen. While the emphasis on formica-topped surfaces might date the play – this is the setting for the opening of Alan Ayckbourn's *Absurd Person Singular*, first performed in 1972 – this is clearly a kitchen which is small but very tidy. It's not a rich kitchen, bristling with every conceivable gadget, but the description stresses the 'gleaming sink unit' and the smart formica-topped and matching surfaces and furniture. This, presumably, is the outward reflection of a tidy, but unimaginative, suburban couple.

The final description, from Arthur Miller's *Death of a Salesman* (1949), is the most detailed. Miller goes beyond mere physical description and seeks to imbue the setting with almost lyrical qualities. The sound of the flute sets the scene and the impression this is meant to convey is given: that of the countryside beyond the city. Instructions for the lighting effects are also stated: the house itself is bathed in blue while the surrounding area has 'an angry glow of orange'. The shapes of the surrounding buildings are 'angular' and as the light grows the apartment houses with their solid fronts seem to threaten the 'small, fragile-seeming home'. All the effects serve to give the impression of a home which is alone, isolated and vulnerable. This is a description beyond a purely realistic one; Miller seeks, through his stage design and his choice of language to describe it, to express emotions above and beyond the 'carpentry' of the set.

In his notes on the set Miller goes on to explain that there are imaginary wall-lines which the actors observe when in the present, but when characters imagine themselves in the past, then these boundaries are broken. The set, then, is more than just the stage representation of a house in the city, but comes to symbolise the daydreams and loss of reality for the main figure, the salesman Willy Loman.

To some playwrights, however, this stylised setting interferes with the characterisation and imposes too strong a message on the how the play is performed and received. The American playwright Sam Shepard describes his set for *True West* (1980) – a kitchen and adjoining alcove of an older home in a southern California suburb – in great detail. He then adds the note that:

> The set should be constructed realistically with no attempt to distort its dimensions, shapes, objects, or colours. No objects should be introduced which might draw special attention to themselves other than the props demanded by the script. If a stylistic 'concept' is grafted onto the set design it will only serve to confuse the evolution of the characters' situation, which is the most important focus of the play.

Directors and designers sometimes feel that a set can 'weigh down' a play and hinder new interpretations; a simple set can 'freshen up' a play and allow both the actors and the audience to focus more on the language.

## Characters

As well as giving instructions for the set playwrights can also describe their characters.

## *Activity*

Read these guidelines on characters, again taken from four different plays. How do these descriptions suggest characterisation?

1   LEN, twenty-one. Tall, slim, firm, bony. Big hands. High, sharp cheek-bones. Pleasant pale complexion – not ashen. Blue eyes, thick fair hair a bit oily, brushed sideways from a parting. Prominent feet.

    PAM, twenty-three. Thin, sharp-busted. Heavy, nodal hips. Dark hair. Long narrow face. Pale eyes. Small mouth. Looks tall from a distance, but is shorter than she looks.

    (Edward Bond's *Saved*)

2   AUSTIN, early thirties, light blue sports shirt, light tan cardigan sweater, clean blue jeans, white tennis shoes.

    LEE, his older brother, early forties, filthy white t-shirt, tattered brown overcoat covered with dust, dark blue baggy suit pants from the Salvation Army, pink suede belt, pointed black forties dress shoes scuffed up, holes in the soles, no socks, no hat, long pronounced sideburns, 'Gene Vincent' hairdo, two days' growth of beard, bad teeth.

    (Sam Shepard's *True West*)

3   When the curtain rises, JANE, a woman in her thirties, is discovered bustling round wiping the floor, cupboard doors, working surfaces – in fact, anything in sight – with a cloth. She sings happily as she works. She wears a pinafore and bedroom slippers, but, under this, a smart new party dress. She is unimaginatively made up and her hair is tightly permed. She wears rubber gloves to protect her hands.

    As Jane works, SIDNEY enters, a small dapper man of about the same age. He has a small trimmed moustache and a cheery, unflappable manner. He wears his best, rather old-fashioned, sober suit. A dark tie, polished hair and shoes complete the picture.

(Alan Ayckbourn's *Absurd Person Singular*)

4    WILLY LOMAN, the Salesman, enters, carrying two large sample cases. The flute plays on. He hears but is not aware of it. He is past sixty years of age, dressed quietly. Even as he crosses the stage to the doorway of the house, his exhaustion is apparent. He unlocks the door, comes into the kitchen, and thankfully lets his burden down, feeling the soreness of his palms. A word-sigh escapes his lips – it might be 'Oh, boy, oh, boy.' He closes the door, then carries his cases out into the living-room, through the draped kitchen doorway.

LINDA, his wife, has stirred in her bed at the right. She gets out and puts on a robe, listening. Most often jovial, she has developed an iron repression of her exceptions to Willy's behaviour – she more than loves him, she admires him, as though his mercurial nature, his temper, his massive dreams and little cruelties, served only as sharp reminders of the turbulent longings within him, longings which she shares but lacks the temperament to utter and follow to their end.

(Arthur Miller's *Death of a Salesman*)

## *Commentary*

As you progress through the examples there is more and more information which points up the personalities of the characters. Indeed, when you come to the final example, from Miller's *Death of a Salesman*, you read character descriptions which could easily have come from a novel. Especially in his portrait of Linda, Miller seeks to fully delineate all the motivation which drives her character. Arguably, such a full exposure of her beliefs and temperament makes the question at the head of the activity redundant; there seems to be little room for an interpretation of her character. Miller's comments are dictatorial and leave little room for manoeuvre for the director and actor. In fact, Linda's role in the play is one of unflinching support for her husband. It is Willy who gets all the good speeches, with enough depth and angst for an actor to get his teeth into.

In stark contrast to Miller's character portraits, the descriptions of Len and Pam from Bond's *Saved* (1965) appear to be solely physical, but carry suggestions of personality traits – for example, 'Pale eyes. Small mouth' suggest something ungenerous. Len's main features seem to be his big hands and prominent feet, which make him appear awkward.

The two descriptions from Shepard's *True West*, on the other hand, are based almost solely on clothes, which reflect the characters' personalities and their lifestyles. The two brothers appear to be quite different; Austin's clean image and light colours contrast with Lee's dirty appearance and preference for dark colours. Nothing seems to match – note the pink suede belt. The indications from the playwright are that Austin cares about his appearance and Lee apparently doesn't.

Ayckbourn, in his descriptions of Jane and Sidney, goes beyond purely outward appearances and gives extra comment on their personalities. He comments, for example, on Jane's actions: she is bustling round, wiping anything in sight and singing happily all the while. And Sidney is described as 'dapper', that is, smart, tidy and neat. With his small trimmed moustache, there seems to be a military aspect about him; he's someone who won't be fazed easily. Jane is allowed a smart new party dress but this is covered with a pinafore. The conservative, unimaginative and sober image which both present nicely matches the description of their kitchen given earlier.

## Exposition

So to the start. Plays need to get the audience's attention from the outset. They often, too, make their intentions known and give some idea of what the audience might expect over the next two hours or so; this is called the **exposition**. Shakespeare employed various ways of opening the drama. In *Hamlet* anxious sentries guard the battlements of a castle at night and wonder whether the ghost of the old king will appear before them, as he has on previous nights. *The Tempest*, not surprisingly, starts with a ship in a storm and all those on board fearful of their safety. *Twelfth Night* has a gentler opening with the lovesick Duke Orsino addressing his musicians with the words: 'If music be the food of love, play on.'

### *Activity*

Perhaps of all the attention-seeking devices, a direct address to the audience is the most obvious. This can be done as a prologue by a chorus figure or by a character in the play. The opening by a chorus figure to Shakespeare's *Romeo and Juliet* certainly makes the nature of its forthcoming action quite clear.

How does this speech set out the nature of the forthcoming action? There is no commentary with this activity.

## Text: *Romeo and Juliet*

> Two households, both alike in dignity,
> In fair Verona, where we lay our scene,
> From ancient grudge break to new mutiny,
> Where civil blood makes civil hands unclean.
> From forth the fatal loins of these two foes
> A pair of star-cross'd lovers take their life;
> Whose misadventur'd piteous overthrows
> Doth with their death bury their parents' strife.
> The fearful passage of their death-mark'd love,
> And the continuance of their parents' rage,
> Which, but their children's end, nought could remove,
> Is now the two hours' traffic of our stage;
> The which if you with patient ears attend,
> What here shall miss, our toil shall strive to mend.

## Openings

At the opening to Arthur Miller's *A View from the Bridge* the lawyer Alfieri who figures throughout the play, both as a character who interacts with other characters and as a character who talks directly to the audience, warns of what is to come:

> every few years there is still a case, and as the parties tell me what the trouble is, the flat air in my office suddenly washes in with the green scent of the sea, the dust in this air is blown away and the thought comes that in some Caesar's year, in Calabria perhaps or on the cliff at Syracuse, another lawyer, quite differently dressed, heard the same complaint and sat there as powerless as I, and watched it run its bloody course.

Plays with a distinct message might well address the audience with a clear indication of the issues involved. Dario Fo's *Accidental Death of an Anarchist* (1970) does just this:

BERTOZZO: (*to audience*) Good evening. I am Inspector Francesco Giovanni Batista Giancarlo Bertozzo of the Security Police. This is my office on the first floor of our notorious headquarters here

**13**

in Milan. Notorious following a sordid little incident a few weeks ago when an anarchist, under interrogation in a similar room a few floors above, fell through the window. Although my colleagues claimed, quite reasonably, that the incident was suicide, the official verdict of the enquiry is that the death of the anarchist was 'accidental'. Bit ambiguous you see. So there's been public outrage, accusations, demonstrations and so on flying around this building for weeks. Not the best atmosphere in which a decent nine to five plainclothes policeman like myself can do an honest inconspicuous day's work.

On the other hand, Bill Naughton's *Alfie* (1963) whose main character is a chirpy, carefree, thirty-something Londoner, opens quite differently:

(*When the curtain rises, the stage is empty.* ALFIE *enters.*)

ALFIE: Are you all settled in nicely? Right, we'll start. My name's . . .
SIDDIE: (*off, in a parked car*) Alfie! Where've you got to?

(*Two short blasts on a car horn are heard*)

ALFIE: (*to the audience*) That's Siddie. She wants me back in the car. Seein' ya.

(ALFIE *exits.*)

The exposition, then, is a setting out of the play's parameters, an indication of what's involved, who's involved, a sense of conflict perhaps, an impending drama, or a waiting for something to happen. Direct address to the audience can easily set the scene. Other ways in to plays which also perform the same function might be characters talking about a situation and perhaps also setting up audience anticipation by mentioning a major character. This certainly happens in *Hamlet* where Horatio talks to the sentries on duty about the current political situation in Denmark. He then makes the point that even though the ghost of the king won't speak to him, he feels sure it will speak to Hamlet. Similarly, at the start of Shakespeare's *Othello* Iago paints a picture of Othello as being proud, loud and lustful. When this image is shattered by Othello's entrance where he calmly and nobly defuses a fight, then we not only feel warm respect for Othello but we also start to doubt the fidelity of what Iago says.

Yet another common way in to a play is the setting up of a situation, characters in readiness for something to happen, a party, a homecoming, or whatever.

Some plays have unusual openings. Peter Shaffer's *Black Comedy* is performed in a reversal of normal light. That is, the first minutes of dialogue are delivered with the stage in complete darkness but the characters are behaving as if they are in normal light. Then the characters experience a blown fuse and lose all light, but for the audience, full stage lights suddenly go on so we can see the characters stumbling around 'in the dark'. This is literally a 'black comedy'.

As for Tom Stoppard's *The Real Inspector Hound*, when this starts, the audience appear to be confronted with their own reflection. We see rows of seats at the back of the stage facing us. In fact this 'play within a play' starts with two theatre critics – Moon and Birdboot – watching a play on the main part of a stage. And throughout its course they comment on the nature of drama and practise their critical reviews for the morning's paper.

First they comment on the opening of the play they've come to review: a kind of whodunnit set in the drawing room of Muldoon Manor, which is cut off from the world on the Essex marshes:

BIRDBOOT:   Yes, well I didn't bring Myrtle tonight – not exactly her cup of tea, I thought, tonight.
MOON:   Over her head, you mean?
BIRDBOOT:   Well, no – I mean it's a sort of *thriller*, isn't it?
MOON:   Is it?
BIRDBOOT:   That's what I heard. Who killed thing? No-one will leave the house.
MOON:   I suppose so. Underneath.
BIRDBOOT:   *Underneath?* It's a whodunnit, man! Look at it!

(*They look at it. The room. The body. Silence.*)

Has it started yet?
MOON:   Yes.

(*A pause. They look at it.*)

BIRDBOOT:   Are you sure?
MOON:   It's a pause.
BIRDBOOT:   You can't start with a *pause!* If you want my opinion there's a total panic back there.

Later in the play Moon speculates on the nature of the drama before him:

MOON:   I think it must be said I am bound to ask – does this play know where it is going? Does it, I repeat, declare its affiliations? There are moments and I would not begrudge it this, when the play, if we can call it that, and I think on balance we can, aligns itself uncompromisingly on the side of life.

## Activity

Read the opening to Cartwright's *Road* and comment on how Cartwright presents Scullery as a character. Note there is no commentary.

## Text: *Road*

(SCULLERY *is on stage or on the floor to greet the audience as they come in. On stage Eddie's Dad is in his house, sitting on an armchair, fixing a Hoover across his knee, the TV on. In another house, Louise's Brother is sitting on a chair fixing an oily engine. Brenda enters her house and sits in an armchair smoking, tense. When all the audience are in and settled, Act 1 begins.*)

(*'Somewhere Over the Rainbow' by Judy Garland is playing. The record ends.*)

(*Blackness.*)

(*A match is struck. It is held underneath a broken road sign. The name part has been ripped off, leaving a sharp, twisted, jagged edge, only the word 'Road' is left. The sign is very old and has been this way a long time.*)

SCULLERY:   It's been broken.

(*The flame moves across to illuminate* SCULLERY's *face. He holds the match there until it goes out; at the same time a spotlight creeps up on his face.*)

Wid' your night yous chose to come and see us. Wid' our night as usual we's all gettin' ready and turning out for a drink. THIS IS OUR ROAD! But tonight it's your road an' all! Don't feel awkward wi' us, make yourselves at home. You'll meet 'all-sorts' down here, I'm telling you love. An' owt can happen tonight. He might get a bird. She might ha' a fight, she might. Let's shove off down t'Road and find out! We'll go down house by house. Hold tight! Here we go! Come on! (*He beckons the audience around.*) Watch the kerb missis! Road's coming round us! (*He starts laughing, laughing uproariously.*)

1   Consider different openings to plays. How quickly do they declare their intentions? For example, compare the openings of some of Shakespeare's comedies.
2   Although not addressed here, endings are obviously important. Good endings signal their coming. How do they do that?
3   Follow up any of the plays to which you've been introduced here; perhaps compare them to plays in similar situations. For example, compare the party situation of Ayckbourn's *Absurd Person Singular* with Mike Leigh's *Abigail's Party*.

# Realism: telling it like it is?

**Realism**

This unit focuses on what is termed naturalistic or realistic drama, that is, drama which is a representation of characters in everyday situations and using apparently real language. **Naturalism** and **realism** are terms which are sometimes used interchangeably, yet they can be confusing. The beginnings of naturalism are associated with the Norwegian playwright Henrik Ibsen. Some of his plays were concerned with social issues in a fairly tight 'family' situation and were designed to be staged in a 'realistic' fashion, that is, an exact replication of a late nineteenth-century middle-class sitting room. Imagine such a room which has one of its walls removed so that the activity of its occupants is on full view to a watching audience. This is the concept of the 'fourth wall': naturalistic theatre, naturalistic acting, naturalistic setting. This kind of theatre was a reaction to what had gone before: theatre which amused and flattered its audiences and which had appropriate acting and language to match. Ibsen's plays dealt with issues which still seem modern and relevant to us today, for example, corruption in politics or the roles of men and women in the family. Realism has been described as an extension or development of naturalism and was a term coined to describe some of the work of the Swedish playwright August Strindberg. His best-known play is *Miss Julie*, which deals with the gulf between the classes and, specifically, the illicit love between the aristocratic Miss Julie and her working-class servant Jean. The issues were dealt with in a more vigorous way – in fact *Miss Julie* was originally banned by the censor as being 'much too risky, much too realistic' but, essentially, both Ibsen and Strindberg were trying to do the same thing: present honestly and openly real concerns for 'real' characters and using 'real' language. Differences between the two styles are marginal and as the term realism easily conjures up the idea of something being realistic, then this seems a more obvious label to apply to drama which tries to 'tell it like it is'.

In England arguably the earliest examples of realistic drama were the so-called **'kitchen sink' dramas** of the 1950s, which departed from the theatre of the day in several ways:

◎ the setting – the action which often would have taken place in a drawing room environment now moved to more 'lived-in' settings, sometimes even the kitchen, hence 'kitchen sink';
◎ the action, following on from more everyday settings, might now feature more everyday activity, for example, making cups of tea, or doing the ironing;
◎ the class of the characters – much more likely to be working class;
◎ the 'issues' – more to do with the nitty-gritty of living;
◎ the language – as appropriate, more likely to be colloquial and informal.

## Activity

In 1965 a storm was raised by Edward Bond's *Saved* which featured the stoning to death of a baby in a pram in a park. Read the opening to the play given here. Referring back to Unit 1, what do you notice about the stage directions here? What is distinctive about the dialogue and what does it tell you about the two characters?

# Text: *Saved*

(*The area of the play is south London. The stage is as bare as possible – sometimes completely bare.*

*The living room. The front and the two side walls make a triangle that slopes to a door back centre.*

*Furniture: table down right, sofa left, TV set left front, armchair up right centre, two chairs close to the table.*

*Empty.*

*The door opens. Len comes in. He goes straight out again.*)

PAM: (*off*) In there.

LEN: (*comes in. He goes down to the sofa. He stares at it.*) All right?

(*Pause.* PAM *comes in.*)

LEN: This ain' the bedroom.

PAM: Bed ain' made.

LEN: Oo's bothered?

PAM: It's awful. 'Ere's nice.

LEN: Suit yourself. Yer don't mind if I take me shoes off? (*He kicks them off.*) No one 'ome?

PAM: No.

LEN: Live on yer tod?

PAM: No.

LEN: O.

(*Pause. He sits back on the couch.*)

Yer all right? Come over 'ere.

PAM: In a minit.

LEN: Wass yer name?

PAM: Yer ain' arf nosey.

LEN: Somethin' up?

PAM: Can't I blow me nose?

(*She puts her hanky back in her bag and puts it on the table.*)

Better.

(*She sits on the couch.*)

LEN: Wass yer name?

PAM: Wass yourn?

LEN: Len.

PAM: Pam.

LEN: O. (*He feels the couch behind with his hand.*) This big enough?

PAM: What yer want? Bligh!

LEN: Don't wan' a push yer off. Shove that cushion up.

PAM: 'Ang on.

LEN: 'Ow often yer done this?

PAM: Don't be nosey.

LEN: Take yer shoes off.

PAM: In a minit.

LEN: Can yer move yer – thass better.

PAM: Yer d'narf fidget.

LEN: I'm okay now.

PAM: Ow!

LEN: D'yer 'ave the light on?

PAM: Suit yerself.

LEN: I ain' fussy.

PAM: Ow!

## Commentary

The bareness of the stage setting indicated by Bond matches the sparse language of the two characters and the bareness of their exchanges. The exchanges are very short and are mostly characterised by a simple question and answer format. Very short responses are given with no expansion, for example:

LEN:   Live on yer tod?
PAM:   No.

The spelling is used to suggest a non-standard variety, in this case, a south London **accent**, for example, 'ave and ain'. The actual **dialect** grammar – that is, choice and arrangement of words – of working-class Londoners is featured, for example 'Yer ain' arf nosey' and 'Yer d'narf fidget', as well as a dialect word like 'tod' meaning, in this context, 'live on your own'.

The characters, then, engage in a restricted minimal exchange of communication. They do not speak in **Standard English** – that is, the form of English used as the standard as found in books, taught to non-native speakers of English and generally used as the benchmark for 'correct' English in schools. Bond gives definite indications of a non-standard dialect; he also indicates the characters' accent through spelling – and this is known as '**eye dialect**'. Their language is colloquial and suggestive of everyday exchanges, but pared down to the minimum to reflect a limited ability to present or explain their feelings.

## Adjacency pairs

Another way to focus on the quality of Pam and Len's exchanges in *Saved* is by examining the structure known as **adjacency pairs**, which underpins much of real conversation. The minimal response needed for a dialogue to take place produces a two-way exchange. Some of the most common two-way exchanges, or adjacency pairs, are:

greeting–greeting                  comment–comment
request–acceptance              offer–acceptance
question–answer

For example:

A:   good morning
B:   morning

Or:

A: lovely day
B: isn't it

Sometimes exchanges are not immediately followed up and other dialogue takes place before the second half of the pair is produced. This is called an **insertion sequence**, as in:

A: what's your age
B: what's yours
A: 18
B: so am I

Here we have a question–answer adjacency pair embedded inside another question and answer pair. A slightly less ordered form of insertion might occur when there is some misunderstanding stopping the expected response. This has to be rectified before the conversation can be resumed. Or, even, the dialogue might wander off on what appears to be a complete side issue before coming back to the required second response; these are called **side sequences**. An example is:

SID:  Right Neil what can I get you?
NEIL:  Er, well . . . thing is, Sid. You know this . . . this voucher you gave Susan for winning the competition?
SID:  Entitling her to a free family meal. Yeah.
NEIL:  I was wondering if . . . like, well . . . if we could sort of . . . cash it in now.
SID:  You want another dinner?
NEIL:  No, no. I mean to pay for the meal we've just had.
SID:  Eh? You've already paid for it.
NEIL:  I know. But . . . I thought you could, you know . . . reimburse us.
SID:  Er, that . . . that wasn't really the idea, Neil.
NEIL:  There's no conditions written on here.
SID:  The whole point is that you come back another day.
NEIL:  Doesn't say when you've got to take the meal.
SID:  I know but . . .
NEIL:  I mean . . . either it's valid for a family meal like it says, or it isn't.
SID:  OK. I suppose . . . give it here. You still have to pay for the drinks. But I'll refund the money for your food on one condition.
NEIL:  What's that?
SID:  You play left midfield tomorrow afternoon.

*(The Archers)*

23

Here, before Neil's request to have the price of his meal refunded is answered both he and Sid embark on a side sequence discussing the concept behind the 'free meal' voucher and the rights and expectations of each party.

Adjacency pairs are so ordered that the first utterance raises expectations of the nature of the second utterance and, by implication, this sets constraints on what the speaker of the second utterance might say. So the use of a question requires an answer, a greeting raises expectations of another greeting, a comment presupposes a similar comment, and so on. It follows, therefore, that where the expected second response is missing then this will suggest that a lack of co-operation is at work, or there is some conflict present, in the hoped-for smooth interaction of conversation.

Looking back at the extract from *Saved* we can see that Len, as the 'guest' in Pam's flat, is doing most of the work in the conversation and setting up most of the exchanges. These are mostly questions and Pam's responses to them vary. If she answers the question directly then her response is the absolute minimum, as in:

LEN:  No one 'ome?
PAM:  No.
LEN:  Live on yer tod?
PAM:  No.

Otherwise she deflects the question back onto Len, as in:

LEN:  This big enough?
PAM:  What yer want? Bligh!

and

LEN:  D'yer 'ave the light on?
PAM:  Suit yerself.

And when Len asks her name Pam initiates a side sequence with 'Yer ain' arf nosey', and when Len tries again, Pam inserts another question–answer adjacency pair of

PAM:  Wass yourn?
LEN:  Len.

before she finally gives her own name as answer to the original question.

There are also two examples of **three part exchanges**. This is where the original speaker follows up the response of the second speaker with some kind of comment or acknowledgement of that response and, again, shows Len doing most of the work in the dialogue, although he utters only the minimum:

LEN:  Live on yer tod?
PAM:  No.
LEN:  O.

and

LEN:  Len.
PAM:  Pam.
LEN:  O.

The seeming realism, then, of the opening extract from *Saved* comes from Bond being able to use our ideas of how conversation works in order to present a particular impression of the speakers. There are very short exchanges with no expansion or development of feelings. There is a difficulty of communication and a lack of social ease. This is shown in the kind of adjacency pairs at work: questions being answered with questions or not being answered at all and this reflects mostly on Pam who seems unwilling, or unable, to commit herself to responding to Len's attentions.

## Activity

The next extract is taken from Caryl Churchill's *Fen* (1983). As the title suggests it is set in rural East Anglia. In this scene Val, who has left her young childen and husband for another man (Frank), is seeking comfort from Shirley who, among other things, works on the land. Geoffrey, also an agricultural labourer, arrives home for dinner. Sometimes a character starts speaking before the other has finished or even continues speaking right through another's speech, and this is marked /. Try reading this out loud. How would you describe the nature of the communication between the two main characters?

## Text: *Fen*

(SHIRLEY's *husband* GEOFFREY, *sixty, comes in. By the end of the scene he has had the soup she prepared.*)

GEOFFREY:  Dinner ready?

SHIRLEY:  Just about.

VAL:  Hello, Geoffrey.

GEOFFREY:  Could do with some dinner.

SHIRLEY:  Ent you got a civil tongue?

GEOFFREY:  I don't hold you personally responsible, Val. You're a symptom of the times. Everything's changing, everything's going down. Strikes, militants, I see the Russians behind it. / All the boys want to do today

SHIRLEY:  You expect too much Val. Till Susan was fifteen I never went out. Geoffrey wouldn't either, he wouldn't go to the pub without me. 'She's mine as much as yours', he says,

GEOFFREY:  is drive their bikes and waste petrol. When we went to school we got beaten and when we got home we got beaten again. They don't want to work today.

SHIRLEY:  'I've as much right to stop in as what you have.'

(*Pause.*)

Lived right out in the fen till ten years ago. You could stand at the door with your baby in your arms and not see a soul from one week's end to the next. / Delivery van come once a week. My sister come at Christmas.

GEOFFREY:  Don't talk to me about unemployment. They've got four jobs. Doing other people out of jobs. Being a horseman was proper work, but all your Frank does is sit on a tractor. Sitting down's not work. Common market takes all the work.

(*Pause.*)

Only twenty in church on Sunday. Declining morals all round. Not like in the war. Those French sending rockets to the Argies, forgotten what we did for them I should think. / Common market's a good thing for stopping wars.

SHIRLEY:  I remember dad said to mum one Bank Holiday, 'Do you want to go out?' 'Yes please,' she said. 'Right,' he said, 'we'll go and pick groundsel.'

GEOFFREY:  We had terrible times. If I had cracked tomatoes for my tea / I thought I was lucky. So why shouldn't you have

SHIRLEY:  It's easy living here like I do now.

GEOFFREY:  terrible times? Who are all these people / who come and live

SHIRLEY:  Your bike'd be mud right up to the middle of the wheel.

GEOFFREY:  here to have fun? I don't know anybody. Nobody does. Makes me wild. / My mother was glad she could

SHIRLEY:  I'd think, 'If anything's after me it'll have to pedal.'

GEOFFREY:  keep us alive, that's all. I'm growing Chinese radishes. I've never eaten Chinese food and I never will. Friend of mine grows Japanese radishes and takes them to Bradford, tries to sell them to the Pakis. Pakis don't want them. You want to pull yourself together, girl, that's what you want to do.

## *Commentary*

The extract opens with a question and answer adjacency pair:

GEOFFREY:  Dinner ready?
SHIRLEY:  Just about

and then Val initiates a greeting–greeting adjacency pair which Geoffrey ignores:

VAL:  Hello, Geoffrey.
GEOFFREY:  Could do with some dinner.

This rudeness is commented on by Shirley who asks:

SHIRLEY:  Ent you got a civil tongue?

Geoffrey has not given the expected response; he has, in effect, broken the 'rules' of co-operating in conversation. As the scene progresses we become aware that Shirley and Geoffrey are almost talking to themselves. Shirley is making the point that Val expects too much from life and then talks of her own experiences in the past. Geoffrey, too, harks back to the past. His views are a mixture of nostalgia and 'popular' prejudice, for example, blaming the Russians for everything or stating that sitting on a tractor isn't real work. There is a seeming rambling quality to his thoughts which perhaps suggests real speech: he says he doesn't blame Val for her actions before commenting on unemployment, the Falklands War, the Common Market and then eventually coming back to telling Val to pull herself together. He also asks questions but doesn't expect, or even want, an answer. The overlapping conversations as each sometimes talks right through the other also suggest real speech and reflect a separateness between them as each takes a different stance on the situation.

## Real conversation at work

Studies in actual conversations have revealed that we do not talk in sentences. Sentence formation and appropriate punctuation are written conventions. Linguists talk about people having turns in conversation and 'sharing the floor'. Conversations often perform a social function – as well as exchanging or giving information, persuading, instructing, entertaining or whatever – and they work on the basis of co-operation and harmony. We assume that what people say to us in conversation is relevant (and true) and we do the same. We negotiate with each other the space and time in which to talk, taking turns in a generally co-operative manner. These turns come at

**completion points** when someone's turn at speaking is finished and the floor is offered to another to take their turn. Completion points are natural ends of statements, or ends of questions, or **tag questions** (literally questions tagged on to the end of statements). A pause at the completion point naturally gives space for another to start.

Looking back at the extract from *Fen*, we can see clearly a lack of co-operation between Shirley and Geoffrey. Neither responds to what the other is saying and they start talking at points which aren't completion points. Moreover, when each pauses and therefore gives space for the other to respond and take over the turn, this offer of a turn is ignored and so the original speaker continues. This serves to highlight their lack of talking or co-operating with each other.

## The co-operative principle

Generally, for conversation to work, we co-operate with each other. To make the negotiation of space and time as harmonious as possible in the 'game' of conversation in which we engage every day, we follow certain rules. Some of these unwritten rules which underpin conversation have been formulated by Paul Grice as the **co-operative principle**. This states that we interpret language on the assumption that speakers are obeying the four maxims of:

1  *quality* (being true)
2  *quantity* (being brief)
3  *relation* (being relevant)
4  *manner* (being clear).

We can break these rules of course, in which case listeners look for reasons why we've done this. Certainly in *Fen* two of the maxims are being ignored: those of quantity and relation. For though Geoffrey believes that what he is saying is true (the maxim of quality), he is not being brief or relevant (that is, ignoring the maxims of quantity and relation). Arguably, Shirley is also breaking the maxim of relation. Focusing on dialogue in this way helps us see how characteristics of speakers are being constructed.

## Soaps

One home of realistic theatre drama is the very popular medium of television soap dramas – called **soaps** because this kind of programme was originally sponsored by soap manufacturers in America – and another, to a lesser extent, is radio dramas. They both have a much more ephemeral nature than theatre drama: a kind of 'throwaway drama', writers produce hours of new material each week. This emotion-driven drama often centres on working-class characters with real everyday concerns. We would expect the dialogue to fairly closely simulate some of the features of real conversation already noted.

## Activity

To what extent does the following extract closely simulate some of the features of real conversation already noted? Make sure you refer to a transcript of a real conversation when doing this. (You could use the transcript in the Introduction.) There is no commentary with this activity.

## Text: *The Archers*

Extract 1: Getting ready for a friendly football match in the village

SID:   Still no sign of him?

TONY:   Apparently he went over to Felpersham to collect some silage. He must have been delayed.

SID:   Oh blimey! He's our main striker! What do we do?

TONY:   Keep stalling, Eddie says. And hope he turns up. If not we'll have to play Neil up front. And put Robert in midfield.

SID:   Terrific!

(*Pause.*)

ROY:   Come on lads, what's the hold up?

SID:   We're not ready.

ROY:   You mean you're trying to hang on till David gets here. Kick off time was five minutes ago, Sid!

SID:   Yeah, alright!

TONY:   It's only a bank holiday kick about, Roy. Not the Cup Final.

ROY:   That's not the point. Kick off's 4 o'clock!

SID:   You're taking it all too seriously.

ROY:   If David's late, it's tough.

TONY:   Yeah, look at you all in your poncy matching red and blue striped kit.

SID:   Where did you get that lot from?

ROY:   Sean got it from a mate.

SID:   Huh! Say no more!

ROY:   Bert . . . can't you do something? They're just trying to waste time till . . .

(*Laughter.*)

SID:   And talking of snappy dressers . . .

TONY:   What are those, Bert? Your pyjamas?

BERT:   It's me referee's gear. Freda's nephew got it for me specially.

TONY:   I thought referees wore black.

BERT: Not at the higher level. You wait till the World Cup. They'll all be wearing kit like this.

Extract 2: During the match

KATE: Oh dear, I think Tony's in trouble.

BERT: Free kick.

TONY: Rubbish!

BERT: Free kick.

TONY: I played the ball!

BERT: Don't argue.

ROY: You were late on him, Tony.

TONY: I got there as soon as I could. He dived, Bert. That's not a free kick.

BERT: I said don't argue.

TONY: I never touched him.

BERT: OK. That's enough!

KATE: What's he doing?

PAM: I think he's . . . yeah it's a yellow card.

TONY: Leave it out, Bert! This is a bit of fun! what are you doing?

BERT: I'm booking you, Tony Archer.

## Extension

1   Collect examples of other contemporary drama written for the stage. How realistic does the language seem? Also how is the class of the characters reflected in their language (and, perhaps, in their concerns, too).

2   Analyse some TV dramas. How closely do the scripts seem to mirror real conversation? Crime series like ITV's *The Bill* do a good job of suggesting real conversation at work. You might want to compare it with other crime programmes set in different parts of the country. Alternatively, you could compare current programmes with past ones, for example, *The Sweeney*. Is it only the hairstyles, clothes and cars which belie their age? Could you date them from their language use alone?

3   Examine other soaps set in different regions. What features mark them out as indicative of their setting? What, beyond the use of flat vowels and the odd dialect feature like the expression 'any road' meaning something like 'anyway', does ITV's *Coronation Street* employ, for instance?

4   Consider radio drama. How does the absence of a picture affect the script?

5   Analyse the following extract from *Coronation Street*. *Coronation Street* scripts are sacrosanct. The writer of this extract, Peter Whalley, has stated that the actors change one word at their peril! It would be useful to come back to this extract after having explored dialect in Unit 3, but, more particularly, cohesion and structure in Unit 5. Certainly, *Coronation Street* scripts would make very fruitful data for investigation work.

## Text: *Coronation Street*

(*The Battersbys' living room.* LES *in his dressing gown, eating cornflakes and watching television, as* JANICE *is preparing to leave for work.*)

LES: Hey, is this right what I were hearing about Rita Sullivan, that she can't remember owt?

JANICE: What they were saying.

LES: Blimey, she's going to have to be careful, running a shop. Handling money and that.

JANICE: At least she has it to handle. We're going to be short in this house, way things are developing over road.

LES: (*Alarmed*) How d'you mean?

JANICE: We're on verge of walking, lot of us.

LES: What're you going to be doing that for?

JANICE: 'Cause of way Mike's sacked Hayley for no reason.

LES: He'll be sacking you, you start your clever tricks. Never mind your walking out. We rely on your wage!

JANICE: Yeah, an' Hayley's relying on us to stand up for her.

LES: Then she's a fool, 'cause everybody looks after theirself in this world.

JANICE: Oh, I'm glad you told me. I shall bear that in mind.

LES: Do that. Just don't come back here telling me you've thrown your job away for some daft bird who hasn't been there two minutes!

(*The Kabin.* RITA *has just served* LES *with cigarettes and is giving him change.*)

RITA: . . . So that's four. Five. And five makes ten.

LES: (*Waits then*) Yeah, only . . . that was a twenty I gave you.

RITA: (*Doesn't think so*) Twenty . . . ?

LES: Yeah.

RITA: Well, no, I don't think it was.

(*As* ALEC *arrives and so will hear.*)

LES: No, honest, Rita. 'Cause, look, that's all I had in me wallet. (*Displaying an empty wallet*) And I'll tell you how I know. 'Cause I remember checking before I came out and thinking I should have got our Jan to sub me. 'Cause a feller needs a bit of walking-around money. But no, she'd gone to work, so I thought oh well, never mind, have to make do. Twenty.

(*But* RITA *has been looking into the till and remains convinced.*)

RITA: And I have a little routine. Which is that, when I'm giving change, I put the note I'm giving change for at the back of the till. And here it is. (*Displaying it*) Ten.

LES: Well, I think your little routine's let you down. 'Cause that was not what I gave you. What I gave you was a twenty.

RITA: Well, I'll tell you what. I'll know when I cash up tonight.

LES: (*Not happy with that*) Are you sure you're not getting confused here, Rita love. I mean I did hear mention that your memory's not what it might be . . .

RITA: (*Resents that*) I am sure, yes. And I'll check it tonight and then we'll both be sure.

LES: Go on then. I suppose I can trust you. (*And heads for the door*)

RITA:  (*Fumes*) I suppose you can.

ALEC:  Would you believe it – I've left me immersion on.

RITA:  You've what?

ALEC:  Back in a tick. (*And hurries out after* LES)

(*The Street.* ALEC *catches up with* LES *who's slowed down to light a fag.*)

ALEC:  Les, Les . . .

LES:  Oh, don't you start. Look, that were a twenty I gave her and now I'm going to be out-of-pocket just 'cause she's wrong in the head!

ALEC:  Yes, yes, I'm not disputing that . . .

(*As he produces a tenner from his own wallet*)

LES:  You're not . . . ?

ALEC:  No, Rita's . . . well, she's had a few difficulties. So this'll make everything straight, will it . . .

LES:  It's very civil of you.

ALEC:  Well, we're put on this earth to help one another, aren't we?

LES:  We are. But there's not everybody sees it like that.

ALEC:  No, well . . .

LES:  So she's still with the fairies then, is she, Rita?

ALEC:  Still recuperating, yes.

# Presentation of character: non-standard language

The last unit focused on texts which attempted to present characters speaking in ways which clearly suggested actual conversation. Of course dramatic texts, whether for the stage or the screen, do have features that mark them as constructed scripts: they have structure, an order, a control which can be seen in the choice of language. As real or naturalistic as they may seem, scripts they quite clearly still remain. They don't contain the non-fluency features of conversation such as fillers, false starts, repetition. Even when playwrights generate a play from improvisation, and also seek to include those 'spontaneous' features in the text, the final script still bears the structure and polish of an obviously written artefact.

As well as attempting to make their dialogue sound more real by replicating some features of conversation, such as short utterances, ellipsis and informal language, some playwrights have gone a stage further and attempted to replicate – or, at least, suggest – some of the features of a regional or ethnic dialect. Everybody has their own individual way of speaking; this is called one's **idiolect**. Idiolect, from the Greek meaning 'personal speech', is a linguistic term for the individual language system of a person: their unique pronunciation, grammatical forms and choice of vocabulary. It consists of the words, or **lexis**, that an individual opts to use – terms of address, perhaps, ways to express delight or anguish, favourite sayings. But idiolect is also the way we pronounce words. Everyone has their own peculiar way of expressing themselves – both in words and sounds. These are the features that entertainers try to replicate when giving impressions of well-known people. Playwrights are perhaps not so much concerned with presenting the language features of one particular individual, as concerned with showing some of the general aspects of a particular community or region. Invariably their portrayal will be generalised. That is, they will utilise a few features which deviate from Standard English; they may also use eye dialect to suggest something of the sound of the words in a particular accent.

# Dialect

Regional speech can be discovered through the sounds we make, the words we use and the grammatical structures we use. In England we might talk of someone as having a northern dialect when we're probably referring to the sound or pronunciation of certain key vowels – their accent. Two differences between north and south of England concern the pronunciation of the 'a' and the 'u' in the middle of words. For example, consider the pronunciations of the words:

> bath     fast     path     graph     bus     cup

Dialect is concerned with the choice and use of words. It's also useful to consider dialect in two different ways: its lexis and its grammar. Lexis is simply the choice of particular words when dealing with semantics or meanings. For example, choices between using:

baby/bairn        ginnel/snicket/alley        wagon/lorry

The **grammar** of a dialect, on the other hand, concerns its way of expressing itself, its syntax or order of words, perhaps. It might also concern its choice of verb forms or its use of the definite article. Examples might be the habit of using tag questions like: 'I missed the bus, didn't I?' which is a grammatical feature of the London dialect. Or, shortening the definite article, which is a common feature of many northern dialects: 'I went to t'shop this morning.' Non-standard verb forms are also common in many dialects, as in: 'We was brilliant at Newcastle. Three nil.'

Early in the twentieth century some British playwrights wanted to write about working-class characters, and at the same time suggest something of their dialect and accent. The Manchester School wanted to create characters (and not the regional caricatures of many people's imaginations). Two important members (with their best-known plays) were Harold Brighouse (*Hobson's Choice*) and Stanley Houghton (*Hindle Wakes*).

*Activity*

Read this extract from *Hindle Wakes* (1912), out loud if possible. Hindle is a working-class mill town in Lancashire and it was traditional for the whole town to close down for a week or two during the summer; these were called Wakes Weeks. In this extract, Christopher has gone up to the mill owner, Jeffcote, because Christopher has just discovered that his daughter Fanny has spent the weekend away with a man – something of a scandal for the time. The two men, by the way, have always been friends. Houghton comments on the Lancashire accent in his foreword to the play but he actually uses standard spelling so no real attempt is made to suggest the accent. Bearing in mind, then, what has been said about dialect, what language features does Houghton use to suggest a Lancashire dialect?

# Text: *Hindle Wakes*

CHRISTOPHER: It's about my lass.

JEFFCOTE: Hullo!

CHRISTOPHER: I'm worried about her.

JEFFCOTE: What's she been doing?

CHRISTOPHER: Getting into trouble.

JEFFCOTE: What sort of trouble?

CHRISTOPHER: (*Troubled.*) Well, thou knows – there's only one sort of trouble –

JEFFCOTE: Ay – ay! With a lad?

CHRISTOPHER: Ay! (*There is a slight pause.*) It's only by chance we found it out. The missus is in a fine way about it, I can tell you!

JEFFCOTE: Then it's proper serious, like?

CHRISTOPHER: They've been away together, these Wakes.

JEFFCOTE: (*Whistling.*) Humph! She's a cool customer. What art going to do in the matter?

CHRISTOPHER: That's what I've come up to see thee about. I wasn't for coming tonight, but missus, she was set on it.

JEFFCOTE: Quite right, too. I'll help thee any road I can. But you mustn't take it too much to heart. It's not the first time a job like this has happened in Hindle, and it won't be the last!

CHRISTOPHER: That's true. But it's poor comfort when it's your own lass that's got into trouble.

JEFFCOTE: There's many a couple living happy today as first come together in that fashion.

CHRISTOPHER: Wedded, you mean?

JEFFCOTE: Ay! Wedded, of course. What else do you think I mean? Does the lad live in Hindle?

CHRISTOPHER: Ay! (*He does not know how to break it to* JEFFCOTE.)

JEFFCOTE: Whose shed does he work at?

CHRISTOPHER: Well, since you put it that way, he works at yours.

JEFFCOTE: At Daisy Bank? Do I know him?

CHRISTOPHER: Ay! You know him well.

JEFFCOTE: Then by Gad! I'll have it out with him tomorrow. If he doesn't promise to wed thy Fanny I'll give him the sack.

CHRISTOPHER: (*Dazed.*) Give him the sack!

JEFFCOTE: And I'll go further. If he'll be a decent lad and make it right with her at once, I'll see that he's well looked after at the mill. We're old pals, Chris, and I can't do fairer than that, can I?

CHRISTOPHER: No.

JEFFCOTE: Now, then, who's the chap?

CHRISTOPHER: Thou'll be a bit surprised-like, I reckon.

JEFFCOTE: Spit it out!

CHRISTOPHER: It's thy lad, Alan.

JEFFCOTE: (*Sharply.*) What? (*A slight pause.*) Say that again.

CHRISTOPHER: Thy lad, Alan.

JEFFCOTE: My lad?

CHRISTOPHER: Ay!

(*After a short pause,* JEFFCOTE *springs up in a blazing rage.*)

JEFFCOTE: Damn you, Chris Hawthorn! Why the devil couldn't you tell me so before?

CHRISTOPHER: I were trying to tell thee, Nat—

JEFFCOTE: Trying to tell me! Hasn't thou got a tongue in thy head that thou mun sit there like a bundle of grey-cloth while I'm making a fool of myself this road?

## *Commentary*

Houghton represents a Lancashire dialect in several ways. First, the lexis. There are a host of words which deviate from the standard. We find:

> lass    lad    ay    missus    road    job

Very common in some regional dialects is the use of 'thou', 'thee' and 'thy' in addition to the standard form 'you'. The former terms indicate informality and are used between parties of equal status, whereas 'you' can indicate distance. So when Jeffcote realises that Fanny has been away with his own son he flares into anger and resorts to the more formal 'you':

> Damn you, Chris Hawthorn! Why the devil couldn't you tell me so before?

The dialect is also reflected in the grammar, that is, the way the characters use verb forms and syntax, the arrangement and order of words. We find non-standard verb forms in:

> art    were    mun

There is the use of the word 'like' which is tagged on after a comment, as in: 'Then it's proper serious, like?', 'Thou'll be a bit surprised-like.'

We find an example of a **tail**, something tagged on to the end of a statement to give emphasis: 'They've been away together, these Wakes.'

Finally, there is the use of 'as' in place of 'who' in: 'There's many a couple living happy today as first come together in that fashion.' And also the particular choice of words which closes the extract: 'I'm making a fool of myself this road.'

## **Standard English**

It's easy to think of Standard English as some kind of neutral way of talking – not a dialect really – and anything that isn't Standard English, therefore, to be a dialect and, by implication, somehow inferior. A dialect, in this case, is just a version of English; Standard English is a dialect like any other. The difference is that, because it was the dialect used by prestigious groups, it became the dominant dialect. Other dialects are different, not wrong or incorrect.

Similarly, some accent features have also acquired prestige. The English language has been changing for hundreds of years and sometimes with no great pattern or consistency. The sounding of the 'r' before consonants or at the end of words, for example, has been an object of fashion. Currently, in England, the sounding of the 'r' does not carry prestige. Therefore we do not value sounding the 'r' at the end of a word like 'car', for example, or the 'r' in a word like 'farm'. Accents which do sound the 'r' in those words – West Country accents, or Norfolk accents, for example – are looked upon by many as 'low-prestige' accents. It encapsulates for some the stereotypical view of the 'country bumpkin.' Yet, in the USA it's the other way round: sounding 'r' carries prestige. You only have to think of the way an American would pronounce 'car' to realise the difference with most city-dwellers in England, who actually don't pronounce the 'r' at the end of the word at all.

The variations in some dialects are often most significant in the level of inflection in verbs. Standard English has evolved so that the **base form** of the verb is used in all cases in the present tense except for the third person singular which adds 's'. For example:

|                     | *base form: eat* | *base form: have* |
| ------------------- | ---------------- | ----------------- |
| 1st person singular | I eat            | I have            |
| 2nd person singular | you eat          | you have          |
| 3rd person singular | he/she *eats*    | he/she *has*      |
| 1st person plural   | we eat           | we have           |
| 2nd person plural   | you eat          | you have          |
| 3rd person plural   | they eat         | they have         |

What many other dialects have done, unlike the Standard, is to regularise all verb forms in the present tense, either to the base form or to the form with 's'. So in one dialect you might find: I eat, you eat, he/she eat and in another dialect I eats, you eats, he/she eats.

## Activity

Arnold Wesker wrote *Roots* in 1959. As he states in his foreword to the play, he was keen to present the dialect and accent of rural Norfolk, without resorting to the clichéd, stereotyped 'country bumpkin' language mocked by city dwellers. In a sense, he goes one step further than the Manchester School writing some fifty years earlier. As well as writing in the dialect of rural working-class Norfolk, he also indicates some of the more prominent features of their accent by using eye dialect spelling. In this extract Beatie Bryant (aged 22) is home on a visit to her parents in their isolated cottage. She has been working in London and is full of the ideas impressed on her by her boyfriend there, called Ronnie.

Read the extract, out loud again if possible, and answer the following questions:

1    How does the dialect differ from Standard English?
2    What accent features does Wesker indicate?
3    What impressions do you get of the characters through the way they speak?

## Text: *Roots*

(*Lunch has just been eaten.* BEATIE *is about to have a bath.*)

MRS BRYANT:  (*To Beatie*) Ask him what he want for his tea.

MR BRYANT:  She don't ever ask me before, what she wanna ask me for now?

MRS BRYANT:  Tell him it's his stomach I'm thinking about – I don't want him complaining to me about the food I cook.

MR BRYANT:  Tell her it's no matters to me – I ent got no pain now besides.

BEATIE:  Mother, is that water ready for my bath?

MRS BRYANT:  Where you hevin' it?

BEATIE:  In the kitchen of course.

MRS BRYANT:  Blust gal, you can't bath in this kitchen during the day, what if someone call at the door?

BEATIE:  Put up the curtain then, I shan't be no more'n ten minutes.

MR BRYANT:  'Sides, who want to see her in her dickey suit.

BEATIE:  I know men as 'ould pay to see me in my dickey suit. (*Posing her plump outline.*) Don't you think I got a nice dickey suit?

(MR BRYANT *makes a dive and pinches her bottom.*)

Ow! Stoppit Bryants, stoppit!

(*He persists.*)

Daddy, stop it now!

MRS BRYANT:  Tell him he can go as soon as he like, I want your bath over and done with.

BEATIE:  Oh Mother, stop this nonsense do. If you want to tell him something tell him – not me.

MRS BRYANT:  I don't want to speak to him, hell if I do.

BEATIE:  Father, get the bath in for me please. Mother, where's them curtains?

(MR BRYANT *goes off to fetch a long tin bath – wide at one end, narrow at the other – while* MRS BRYANT *leaves washing up to fish out some curtains which she hangs from one wall to another concealing thus a corner of the kitchen.*)

BEATIE:  I'm gonna wear my new dress and go across the fields to see Frankie and Pearl.

MRS BRYANT:  Frankie won't be there, what you on about? He'll be gettin' the harvest in.

BEATIE:   You makin' anything for the harvest festival?

MR BRYANT:   (*Entering with bath, places it behind curtain*) Your mother don't ever do anything for the harvest festival – don't you know that by now.

BEATIE:   Get you to work father Bryant, I'm gonna plunge in water and I'll make a splash.

MRS BRYANT:   Tell him we've got kippers for tea and if he don' want none let him say now.

BEATIE:   She says it's kippers for tea.

MR BRYANT:   Tell her I'll eat kippers. (*Goes off, collecting bike on the way.*)

BEATIE:   He says he'll eat kippers. Right now, Mother, you get cold water an' I'll pour the hot.

(*The bath is prepared with much childlike glee.* BEATIE *loves her creature comforts and does with unabashed, almost animal, enthusiasm that which she enjoys.*)

MRS BRYANT:   You hear about Jimmy Skelton? They say he's bin arrested for accosting some man in the village.

BEATIE:   Jimmy Skelton what own the pub?

MRS BRYANT:   That's him. I know all about Jimmy Skelton though. He were a young boy when I were a young girl. I always partner him at whist drives. He's been to law before you know. Yes! An'

he won the day too! Won the day he did. I don't take notice though, him and me gets on all right. What do Ronnie's mother do with her time?

BEATIE:   She's got a sick husband to look after.

MRS BRYANT:   She an educated woman?

BEATIE:   Educated? No. She's a foreigner. Nor ent Ronnie educated neither. He's an intellectual, failed all his exams. They read and things.

MRS BRYANT:   Oh, they don't do nothing then?

BEATIE:   Do nothing? I'll tell you what Ronnie do, he work till all hours in a hot ole kitchen. An' he teach kids in a club to act and jive and such. And he don't stop at week ends either 'cos then there's political meetings and such and I get breathless trying to keep up wi' him. OOOhh, Mother it's hot . . .

MRS BRYANT:   I'll get you some cold then.

BEATIE:   No – ooh – it's lovely. The water's so soft Mother.

MRS BRYANT:   Yearp.

BEATIE:   It's so soft and smooth. I'm in.

MRS BRYANT:   Don't you stay in too long gal. There go the twenty-minutes-past-one bus.

BEATIE:   Oh Mother, me bath cubes. I forgot me bath cubes. In the little case by me pick-up.

*Commentary*

The most frequent difference between this Norfolk dialect and Standard English concerns the use of the base form of the verb in the present tense for the third person singular – fifteen instances, in fact. The first two examples occur in the first exchange between Mrs and Mr Bryant (although they are 'talking' to each other through Beatie):

MRS BRYANT:   (*To Beatie*) Ask him what he *want* for his tea.
MR BRYANT:    She *don't* ever ask me before, what she wanna ask me for now?

Other features of the Norfolk dialect can be seen in the omission of the definite article, as in:

BEATIE:   Get you to work father Bryant, I'm gonna plunge in water and I'll make a splash.

Standard English would say: 'plunge in *the* water'. There are also instances of what is called the double negative, for example:

MRS BRYANT:   Tell him we've got kippers for tea and if he *don'* want *none* let him say now.

Standard English would use either: 'if he doesn't want any' or ' if he wants none'. Interestingly, the history of the double negative in some dialects – London, as well as this Norfolk dialect – is the reverse of the change towards base form. As far as we know, all dialects of English once used the double negative; it can be found in Shakespeare, for example. However, in Standard English its use gradually died out; but in many other dialects this change did not happen and so it remains in use. Arguments put forward that it must be incorrect because 'two negatives cancel each other out' don't really hold water. One could quite easily argue that a double negative adds emphasis; furthermore they are the norm in French and Spanish.

As far as indications of some aspects of the accent are concerned, these are mostly concentrated in some amendments of the 'a' vowel in words like: 'ain't' and 'havin''. The eye dialect spelling suggests how they should sound, so: 'ent' and 'hevin''. Wesker also indicates that an 'r' sound creeps into the colloquial 'yep' so that it sounds like 'yearp'.

There are other various features that you might have picked out, especially when Mrs Bryant embarks on her story about Jimmy Skelton.

All these features, then, clearly mark the dialect out as being non-standard. Some may see this as 'quaint'; it may reinforce a stereotype of rural folk as being slow or dim-witted. You may, however, feel that the characters' dialect suggests a sincere, unpretentious people; the horse play between Beatie and her father perhaps reinforces this. Simple by nature and inhabiting a world where the punctuality of the local bus is fairly crucial, Mrs Bryant yet has the perception to see what Ronnie is really like much more so than her daughter.

BEATIE:   He's an intellectual, failed all his exams. They read and things.
MRS BRYANT:   Oh, they don't do nothing then?

And although concerned with what Ronnie might like to eat when he comes, in fact he never does come. Beatie discovers, later than most, that Ronnie is a talker and not a doer. In some ways he fulfils another stereotype: that of the city boy, too consumed with his own importance.

**four**

# The Shakespearean protagonist

The last unit focused on ways that playwrights sought to delineate quite specifically the way that their characters spoke – by suggesting not only the choice of words or grammar employed but also how some of the dialogue might actually sound. This fourth unit will look at the language used by main characters, often *the* main character in a play. A main character may be referred to as the **protagonist** – from the Greek meaning the 'first actor' – sometimes used synonymously with 'hero'. A play strictly speaking would have only one protagonist; however, some plays may either not have an obvious 'main' character, or, if they do, the main character may seem to be more of an 'anti-hero', that is, someone not of noble birth – not a king, perhaps – and someone too greatly flawed to be thought of as a hero; someone unable to perform acts of bravery, perhaps.

## The soliloquy

Some well-known protagonists that come to mind might be the eponymous heroes of Shakespeare's *Hamlet*, *Macbeth* or *Othello* and a vehicle for their thoughts and motivation was the **soliloquy**. This unique dramatic device allows the character to detail their innermost thoughts, revealing more than could be gathered from the action of the play alone. It's as if we are eavesdropping on them talking to themselves; they might be making some kind of statement or engaging in an internal debate.

## *Activity*

Here is a fairly typical example, from near the end of *Macbeth*. Macbeth is preparing for a fight to the death. His soliloquy is a philosophical comment, a statement, about fears and life and death. Read the text and then answer the following questions:

1    How does he talk of his senses to explain his experience of fear?
2    What repetition can you find – of words or ideas?
3    What does Macbeth compare life to?

## Text: *Macbeth*

(*A cry of women is heard off stage.*)

MACBETH:   I have almost forgot the taste of fears.
   The time has been, my senses would have cool'd
   To hear a night-shriek, and my fell of hair
   Would at a dismal treatise rouse and stir
   As life were in't. I have supp'd full with horrors;
   Direness, familiar to my slaughterous thoughts,
   Cannot once start me.

(*Enter* SEYTON)

   Wherefore was that cry?
SEYTON:   The Queen, my lord, is dead.
MACBETH:   She should have died hereafter;
   There would have been a time for such a word.
   To-morrow, and to-morrow, and to-morrow,
   Creeps in this petty pace from day to day,
   To the last syllable of recorded time;
   And all our yesterdays have lighted fools
   The way to dusty death. Out, out, brief candle!
   Life's but a walking shadow, a poor player,
   That struts and frets his hour upon the stage,
   And then is heard no more. It is a tale
   Told by an idiot, full of sound and fury,
   Signifying nothing.

## *Commentary*

Macbeth's first lines are a comment on the cry of women and the fact that he is no longer disturbed by fears. He explains his experience of fears through his senses. He talks of:

taste    senses    hear    supp'd

He also uses words with similar meanings:

fears    horrors    direness    slaughterous

The effect is to emphasise the horror, the fear. When he learns that his queen is dead Macbeth comments on the futility of life: he compares life to a briefly lit candle and to a poor actor, briefly seen on stage and then heard no more. In doing this he draws on three ideas, to do with time, light/dark and acting, as follows:

| *Time* | *Light* | *Acting* |
|---|---|---|
| time | lighted | player |
| tomorrow | candle | stage |
| pace | shadow | tale |
| day | | |
| yesterdays | | |
| hour | | |

Shakespeare is using imagery about time, about light and about acting in order to comment on the shortness of life and its pointlessness: like a brief but meaningless play. And death is the darkness at the end of this play, when the light goes out. This comparing of unlike things is an example of metaphorical language. Metaphor is one of the most common characteristics of literary language. **Metaphor** (from the Greek meaning 'a carrying over') takes comparison to its logical conclusion by saying that one thing *is* another. To take another example from *Macbeth* – earlier in the play Macbeth considers the consequences of killing his king and decides that he has no right to do so:

I have no spur
To prick the sides of my intent, but only
Vaulting ambition, which o'erleaps itself,
And falls on th'other.

He is saying that ambition is his only motive but this will fail him, like a horse which jumps too high and falls. (See also Unit 5 for more examples of figurative language.) **Direct repetition** is also effective in reinforcing Macbeth's thoughts. We get emphasis from:

> day to day
> Out, out
> To-morrow, and to-morrow, and to-morrow

The last example is particularly effective; this repetition in threes is called a three part list and is further explored, again, in Unit 5.

The linking of similar imagery in Macbeth's speech gives us areas of **semantic fields**, that is, drawing on words of similar meaning or from the same area of meaning. Another way, then, of describing how the power of Macbeth's language works is to say that he draws on the semantic fields of:

> senses       horror       time       light       acting

Words from the same semantic field give emphasis and increase the effect of what is being said. In some ways this is another form of repetition.

## *Activity*

Perhaps the most famous soliloquy of all is Hamlet's 'To be, or not to be' speech. In this soliloquy he is considering the pros and cons of whether to tackle the problems of the current situation or leave them. This leads him on to the reflection that it's only the fear of the unknown (after death) that makes us continue to suffer all kinds of things here in life. Shakespeare takes the statement-like soliloquy of Macbeth a stage further. Hamlet's soliloquy is more of an argument; we see his thought processes at work as ideas and words trigger further thoughts.

◎    Isolate the different semantic fields at work.
◎    Comment on Hamlet's use of questions.
◎    Trace Hamlet's line of thought in this speech.

## Text: *Hamlet* 1

To be, or not to be, that is the question:
Whether 'tis nobler in the mind to suffer
The slings and arrows of outrageous fortune,
Or to take arms against a sea of troubles,
And by opposing end . . . them. To die, to sleep –
No more and by a sleep to say we end
The heart-ache and the thousand natural shocks
That flesh is heir to; 'tis a consummation
Devoutly to be wish'd. To die, to sleep –
To sleep, perchance to dream – ay, there's the rub,
For in that sleep of death what dreams may come,
When we have shuffled off this mortal coil,
Must give us pause; there's the respect
That makes calamity of so long life:
For who would bear the whips and scorns of time,
Th'oppressor's wrong, the proud man's contumely,[1]
The pangs of despis'd love, the law's delay,
The insolence of office, and the spurns
That patient merit of th'unworthy takes,
When he himself might his quietus make
With a bare bodkin;[2] who would fardels bear,
To grunt and sweat under a weary life,
But that the dread of something after death,
The undiscover'd country, from whose bourn[3]
No traveller returns, puzzles the will,
And makes us rather bear those ills we have,
Than fly to others that we know not of?
Thus conscience does make cowards of us all,
And thus the native hue of resolution
Is sicklied o'er with the pale cast of thought,
And enterprises of great pitch and moment
With this regard their currents turn awry,
And lose the name of action.

*Notes:* 1 contumely = arrogant speech or behaviour.
2 his quietus make with a bare bodkin = take his own life (quietus) with nothing but a dagger (bodkin); quietus = also a legal term which released an accountant from being responsible for the accounts he was working on.
3 bourn = boundary.

The three main semantic fields concern the areas of sleep/dreams/death, law and travel. To a large extent, too, these three fields underline Hamlet's thoughts and help structure his speech. Also as he develops his thinking he asks **rhetorical questions** – questions that need no answer – and balances these with statements and comments. His thoughts about death – sometimes called the big sleep – make him think about dreams and whether death is the end of everything or whether (like dreams in sleep) there is something after death. He uses figurative language to compare the state after death like a country to which one travels, but never to return. This is the unknown:

> The undiscover'd country, from whose bourn
> No traveller returns

The central part of his speech is concerned with the toils or unfairness of life and he emphasises this with a list partly drawn from the field of law:

> Th'oppressor's wrong
> the law's delay
> The insolence of office
> quietus

Although this soliloquy is meant to reflect Hamlet's own thoughts as he thinks through his position, the way it makes its points is rather like that of a persuasive speech. It asks rhetorical questions, it draws on semantic fields. It uses direct repetition – 'die' and 'sleep' – and it uses a list:

> For who would bear the whips and scorns of time,
> Th'oppressor's wrong, the proud man's contumely,
> The pangs of despis'd love, the law's delay,
> The insolence of office, and the spurns
> That patient merit of th'unworthy takes

All these features help in conveying the powerful effect of Hamlet's thoughts. But, perhaps, most emphatically of all, it starts with a – very famous – **contrasting pair**:

> To be, or not to be

where the second half of the utterance mirrors and neatly balances the first.

This device gets attention and concisely summarises Hamlet's position. Much more recently Neil Armstrong used the same device to encapsulate the achievement of the first human to walk on the moon:

> that's one small step for a man
> one giant leap for mankind.

## Activity

So far in this unit you have looked at protagonists in Shakespeare. Iago, in *Othello*, can be seen as the **antagonist** – the opponent to the protagonist – and he also has several soliloquies where he outlines his position and thinks through his plans.

Read carefully the soliloquy on page 51, where Iago talks of various things: his views of other characters; his own motives; his future plans. Comment on how Shakespeare presents these different ideas.

That Cassio loves her, I do well believe't;
That she loves him, 'tis apt and of great credit.
The Moor (howbeit that I endure him not)
Is of a constant, loving, noble nature
And I dare think he'll prove to Desdemona
A most dear husband. Now I do love her too,
Not out of absolute lust (though peradventure
I stand accountant for as great a sin).
But partly led to diet my revenge,
For that I do suspect the lustful Moor
Hath leap'd into my seat; the thought whereof
Doth (like a poisonous mineral) gnaw my inwards;
And nothing can or shall content my soul
Till I am even'd with him, wife for wife;
Or failing so, yet that I put the Moor
At least into a jealousy so strong
That judgement cannot cure. Which thing to do,
If this poor trash of Venice, whom I trace
For his quick hunting, stand the putting on,
I'll have our Michael Cassio on the hip,
Abuse him to the Moor in the rank garb
(For I fear Cassio with my night-cap too),
Make the Moor thank me, love me, and reward me,
For making him egregiously an ass,
And practising upon his peace and quiet
Even to madness. 'Tis here; but yet confus'd,
Knavery's plain face is never seen till us'd.

## *Activity*

Analyse these words of Othello as he approaches his wife Desdemona, in bed asleep, with the intention of killing her:

## Text: *Othello 2*

(*Enter* OTHELLO *with a light*)

It is the cause, it is the cause, my soul;
Let me not name it to you, you chaste stars,
It is the cause. Yet I'll not shed her blood,
Nor scar that whiter skin of hers than snow,
And smooth as monumental alabaster.
Yet she must die, else she'll betray more men.
Put out the light, and then put out the light:
If I quench thee, thou flaming minister,
I can again thy former light restore,
Should I repent me; but once put out thy light,
Thou cunning'st pattern of excelling nature,
I know not where is that Promethean[1] heat
That can thy light relume. When I have pluck'd thy rose,
I cannot give it vital growth again,
It must needs wither. I'll smell thee on the tree. (*Kisses her*)
A balmy breath, that dost almost persuade
Justice to break her sword![2] One more, one more.
Be thus when thou art dead, and I will kill thee
And love thee after. One more, and that's the last.
So sweet was ne'er so fatal. I must weep,
But they are cruel tears. This sorrow's heavenly,
It strikes when it doth love. She wakes.

*Notes:* 1 Promethean = Prometheus, who brought fire down to mankind from heaven.
2 the sword and scales were emblems of Justice.

# Storytelling

As far as we can tell drama, as we understand it, started out as storytelling. Certainly in the early Greek period stories would be recounted chorus-style; and someone stepping out of the chorus to narrate, or act, formed the first actor, or protagonist, of the drama. In England the earliest forms of drama were the religious Mystery Plays. This was a way to en-act the stories of the Bible for a mostly illiterate audience. The first unit talked of drama as two people plus a passion on a stage. Perhaps to that we should add – 'plus a story' – unless, of course, the passion is seen as a dramatic form of story. We should also, at this point, draw attention to two different kinds of story. One is the story of the whole play – the exposition, the events, the interaction of the characters, the conclusion. The other kind of story concerns the form of storytelling itself. That is, a character telling a story or explaining, through a story, their position or motivation for doing something. It is this latter form of individual story with which we are concerned here.

A character's story can form the whole dialogue of a play. Alan Bennett's monologues do this; so does Samuel Beckett's *Krapp's Last Tape*. More normally, perhaps, characters tell stories for other characters in the play. We probably take stories for granted, meaning we listen for their salient points and assume the teller has a good reason for narrating the story. We probably also assume that stories have a beginning and an end. But stories can be quite varied and use language in quite different ways. Work done on actual everyday storytelling can be illuminating in helping us examine the various stages that stories go through.

## Labov's narrative categories

William Labov (1972) collected stories from New York Black English vernacular culture and, as a result, suggested that fully-formed oral narratives had the following six-part structure:

1   *Abstract*: signals the start of the story, gets the listener's attention and perhaps gives some indication of what the story is about.
2   *Orientation*: sets the scene, gives the time, place, person(s) involved and situation/activity; the 'when, where, who and what?' of the story.
3   *Complicating Action*: the main events of the story, normally in chronological order.
4   *Resolution*: the final event(s) of the story.
5   *Evaluation*: comments on the story, why it's being told, why it's important.
6   *Coda*: signals that the story has finished.

Of course, not all stories are necessarily so neatly ordered or fully-formed. A story could quite easily start without an Abstract; or the Abstract and Orientation might be one and the same thing, e.g. 'It was last summer . . .'. But generally speaking, Labov's order of categories holds good. Evaluation, however, is a kind of 'time out' from the episodic telling of the story. It covers anything and everything that isn't part of the re-telling of events. Comments by the speaker on the story that they are telling, or voicing what the story means to them, would all count as evaluation. Consequently, Evaluation can occur at any point in the story.

## Activity

Read this example of an oral narrative. How far does it follow Labov's categories? Note ½ second pauses are indicated by (.) and one second pauses by (1).

## Text: *Gabriel's story*

well Gabriel (.) who's a little on the impulsive side (.) met this bloke when she was sixteen (.) moved in with him the next day but that's beside the point (.) she met this bloke on Saturday night (.) he said ooooh come out to the pub like on Sunday lunchtime (.) so she went out (.) started drinking with this sort of rugger-bugger type (.)

so eight pints later she was in the curry house like this (.) and she funnily enough she slumped over her chicken tikka or whatever (.) and erm what they did all these ten blokes hid round the corner like in the kitchen of the curry house and they got the manager to come and wake her up and say all your mates have gone (.) you've got a hundred quid bill (.) you've got to pay (1) she'd only met this bloke the night before (1)

and she was going like (.) oh my God I haven't got anything here (.) take my jewellery (.) take my watch (.) I'll (.) I'll come back with the money as soon as I've been to the bank later (.) he was going no no I'm not going to let you leave the premises (.) I'm going to call the police (.) all this sort of stuff (1)

anyway they waited till she was on the point of hysterics and they all came out going ha ha what a good joke (.) like this (.) it's not a very nice story is it (.) she's still with him (.) that's four years later (.) and that's his bloody nicest feature (.) that's the nicest story she can tell about him

## Commentary

The story about Gabriel starts with just one word of Abstract, 'well', then gives Orientation: who? when? and where? 'Gabriel . . . this bloke . . . Saturday night/Sunday lunchtime . . . the pub'. There's Evaluation, too: 'a little on the impulsive side . . . moved in with him the next day but that's beside the point'.

The story proper, the Complicating Action, starts at: 'so she went out' and ends at the Resolution of: 'anyway they waited till she was on the point of hysterics and they all came out going ha ha what a good joke'. The Coda 'that's the nicest story she can tell about him' signals the end of the story. The narrator gives further Evaluation in: 'she'd only met this bloke the night before . . . all this sort of stuff . . . it's not a very nice story is it (.) she's still with him (.) that's four years later (.) and that's his bloody nicest feature'.

There are other non-fluency features common to unscripted talk. For example: fillers – 'erm'; a false start – 'I'll (.) I'll come back'; and a form of hedge (see below): 'like this . . . like . . . like this'.

Labov was trying to find a structure for spontaneously occurring oral narratives, and not analysing stories spoken by characters in plays. However, it can be interesting to apply his categories to a scripted story from drama to see whether they apply at all to a written form that is meant to be spoken; and whether their presence can tell us anything about how 'real' the story seems.

## Activity

Read the extract opposite from Arthur Miller's *Death of a Salesman*. In this crucial speech Willy Loman, the protagonist of the play, is explaining to his young boss why he became a salesman.

Divide Willy's story according to Labov's categories. Make sure, also, that you separate the bare bones of the story – the 'what actually happened' elements – from Willy's comments.

Now read the text opposite.

## Commentary

Willy's story clearly starts with an Abstract: 'Just let me tell you a story, Howard.' He then proceeds to give Orientation for his story, setting the scene of how he was thinking of going to join his father in Alaska. Then the story proper starts – the Complicating Action – with the lines: 'And I was almost decided to go, when I met a salesman in the Parker House.'

The Resolution, the final event of the story, which for Willy is very important, is: 'when he died, hundreds of salesmen and buyers were at his funeral'. Willy's story also clearly ends with the Coda: 'They don't know me any more.'

If you separate out the actual events of the story from Willy's comments, then you find his feelings about what he's saying, his Evaluation of his story. So lines such as the following clearly reveal Willy's deep concern for the way things are, or, at least, seem to be to him:

I'll never forget

And when I saw that, I realized that selling was the greatest career a man could want. 'Cause what could be more satisfying than to be

# Text: *Death of a Salesman*

> WILLY: (*desperately*) Just let me tell you a story, Howard. When I was a boy – eighteen, nineteen – I was already on the road. And there was a question in my mind as to whether selling had a future for me. Because in those days I had a yearning to go to Alaska. See, there were three gold strikes in one month in Alaska, and I felt like going out. Just for the ride, you might say. My father lived many years in Alaska. He was an adventurous man. We've got quite a streak of self-reliance in our family. I thought I'd go out with my older brother and try to locate him, and maybe settle in the North with the old man. And I was almost decided to go, when I met a salesman in the Parker House. His name was Dave Singleman. And he was eighty-four years old, and he'd drummed merchandise in thirty-one states. And old Dave, he'd go up to his room, y'understand, put on his green velvet slippers – I'll never forget – and pick up his phone and call the buyers, and without ever leaving his room, at the age of eighty-four, he made his living. And when I saw that, I realized that selling was the greatest career a man could want. 'Cause what could be more satisfying than to be able to go, at the age of eighty-four, into twenty or thirty different cities, and pick up a phone, and be remembered and loved and helped by so many different people? Do you know? When he died – and by the way he died the death of a salesman, in his green velvet slippers in the smoker of the New York, New Haven, and Hartford, going into Boston – when he died, hundreds of salesmen and buyers were at his funeral. Things were sad on a lotta trains after that. In those days there was personality in it, Howard. There was respect, and comradeship, and gratitude in it. Today, it's all cut and dried, and there's no chance for bringing friendship to bear – or personality. You see what I mean? They don't know me any more.

able to go, at the age of eighty-four, into twenty or thirty different cities, and pick up a phone, and be remembered and loved and helped by so many different people?

In those days there was personality in it, Howard. There was respect, and comradeship, and gratitude in it. Today, it's all cut and dried, and there's no chance for bringing friendship to bear – or personality.

The fact that the Evaluation is almost as long as the story proper reflects Willy's angst and his wish to explain himself.

Willy's story, then, does seem to follow the pattern found in actually occurring oral narratives. Another feature of interest is his use of:

y'understand
Do you know?
You see what I mean?

These are examples of **hedges**, features found in spontaneous conversation and used to get the listener to share in the opinion voiced by the speaker. Their presence further helps to suggest the naturalness of Willy's story.

# Cohesion

Of course, at the end of the day, we *are* dealing with script, written by playwrights. The main difference between spontaneous speech and scripted speech lies in an overall sense of structure and an internal sense of **cohesion**. Cohesion, like glue, is what links text together. It gives text a fluency – indeed, we can talk of a well-written text as being cohesive – and helps to make it coherent. It can function within a sentence and across or between sentences.

**Lexical cohesion** concerns links in the meanings or semantics of words. Direct repetition and synonym repetition are the two most common examples. For instance, looking back at Willy Loman's speech above we can find several links:

> Alaska – Alaska – Alaska – the North
> father – man – old man
> salesman – Dave Singleman – old Dave
> eighty-four – eighty-four – eighty-four
> buyers – people – buyers
> died – died – death – died

It's perhaps obvious that these words should be repeated in a story about the death of a salesman; none the less they all help to tie the text tightly together.

We can also distinguish another form of cohesion, less concerned with meanings of words and more concerned with shaping or joining sentences: this is **grammatical cohesion**. The three most important features concern the use of: conjunctions, syntax repetition and pronoun reference.

Willy Loman's speech, first, is clearly held together by conjunctions: several 'ands', a 'because' and a ''cause'. This helps the speech flow naturally as Willy adds the various points important to him about the old salesman. Then, towards the end of his story, we find syntax repetition in:

> there was personality
> there was respect
> there's no chance

where the two positive statements about what 'there was' in the past are negated by the statement of what 'there is' in the present.

Pronouns, replacing nouns, also help bridge across sentences. They can be used extensively. Take the following example:

> My father lived many years in Alaska. *He* was an adventurous man. We've got quite a streak of self-reliance in our family. I thought I'd go out with my older brother and try to locate *him*, and maybe settle in the North with the old man.

'He' and 'him' only make sense because earlier the subject of 'my father' was introduced. These two pronouns refer back to the noun 'father'. This referring back to an earlier word is called **anaphoric reference**. There are similar references made back to the 'salesman' with 'his' and 'he'. Again, perhaps these ties can be seen as obvious features but they all help to knit together a text and, as such, are clear features of a written script.

## *Activity*

This next extract is taken from *Her Big Chance*, an Alan Bennett monologue. Here, Lesley, a small-time actor, is describing her experiences on set. What do the choices of language tell us about her character? What repetition can you find? Can you describe its effect? And can you say how this contributes to the humour?

# Text: *Her Big Chance*

Please don't misunderstand me. I've no objection to taking my top off. But Travis as I was playing her wasn't the kind of girl who would take her top off. I said, 'I'm a professional, Nigel. Credit me with a little experience. It isn't Travis.' I'd been sitting on the deck of the yacht all day as background while these two older men had what I presumed was a business discussion. One of them, who was covered in hair and had a real weight problem, was my boyfriend apparently. You knew he was my boyfriend because at an earlier juncture you'd seen him hit me across the face. Travis is supposed to be a good-time girl, though you never actually see me having a good time, just sat on this freezing cold deck plastering on the sun tan lotion. I said to Nigel, 'I don't know whether the cameraman's spotted it, Nigel, but would I be sunbathing? There's no sun.' Nigel said, 'No sun is favourite.' Nigel's first assistant, here there and everywhere. Gunther never speaks, not to me anyway. Just stands behind the camera with a little cap on. Not a patch on Roman. Roman had a smile for everybody.

Anyway, I'm sitting there as background and I say to Nigel, 'Nigel, am I right in thinking I'm a denizen of the cocktail belt?' He said, 'Why?' a bit guardedly. I said, 'Because to me, Nigel, that implies a cigarette-holder,' and I produced quite a modest one I happened to have brought with me. He went and spoke to Gunther, only Gunther ruled there was to be no smoking. I said, 'On grounds of health?' Nigel said, 'No. On grounds of it making continuity a bugger.' I'd also brought a paperback with me just to make it easier for props (which seemed to be Scott again). Only I'd hardly got it open when Nigel relieved me of it and said they were going for the sun tan lotion. I said, 'Nigel, I don't think the two are incompatible. I can apply sun tan lotion and read at the same time. That is what professionalism means.' He checked with Gunther again and he came back and said, 'Forget the book . Sun tan lotion is favourite.' I said, 'Can I ask you something else?' He said, 'Go on.' I said, 'What is my boyfriend discussing?' He said, 'Business.' I said, 'Nigel. Would I be right in thinking it's a drugs deal?' He said, 'Does it matter?' I said, 'It matters to me. It matters to Travis. It helps my character. He said, 'What would help your character is if you took your bikini top off.' I said, 'Nigel. Would Travis do that?' I said, 'We know Travis plays chess. She also reads. Is Travis the type to go topless?' He said, 'Listen. Who do you think you're playing, Emily Brontë? Gunther wants to see your knockers.'

I didn't even look at him. I just took my top off without a word and applied sun tan lotion with all the contempt I could muster. They did the shot, then Nigel came over and said Gunther liked that and if I could give him a whisker more sensuality it might be worth a close-up. So we did it again and then Nigel came over and said Gunther was liking what I was giving them and in this next shot would I slip off my bikini bottom. I said, 'Nigel. Trust me. Travis would not do that.' Talks to Gunther. Comes back. Says Gunther agrees with me. The real Travis wouldn't. But by displaying herself naked before her boyfriend's business associate she is showing her contempt for his whole way of life. I said, 'Nigel. At last Gunther is giving me something I can relate to.' He says, 'Right! Let's shoot it! Elbow the bikini bottom!'

## Commentary

This is clearly a very different piece to the extract from *Death of a Salesman*. It's really a three-character scene experienced through the eyes and ears of one of them. Lesley reports what happened on set, faithfully and virtually without comment, or Evaluation. She also speaks directly to the audience, reporting artlessly, or without real understanding of what's going on. As it is, we can clearly see how she is viewed, and treated, by Nigel and Gunther – an example of dramatic irony.

## Structure

The extract is clearly tightly scripted. If we focus on the content of the structure we can see a clear pattern. We start with a comment from Lesley who is unhappy about her character, Travis, taking her top off: 'But Travis as I was playing her wasn't the kind of girl who would take her top off.' Yet, by the end, Lesley is agreeing to total nudity because Gunther gives her character motivation. When an idea or subject is introduced early on, only to be returned to later, then this is called a **plant**. It's as if a seed of an idea has been sown, only to resurface later. Plants can be laid at the beginnings of whole plays – and frequently are – and can form the basis for underlying themes. Lesley's so-called 'professionalism' and experience also run throughout the text. She is continually suggesting 'improvements' for her character, and continually she is being slapped down; they just want her to take her clothes off.

The extract relies heavily on **embedded speech** – the quoting of dialogue within a story; and, even when direct speech isn't reported some of the lines mimic dialogue, for example: 'Says Gunther agrees with me. The real Travis wouldn't. But by displaying herself naked before her boyfriend's business associate she is showing her contempt for his whole way of life.' We even find what looks like Gunther's possible Germanic use of English – 'Gunther was liking'.

As far as repetition goes, perhaps the examples that stand out the most concern syntax repetition:

I said
Nigel/he said
I said, 'Nigel . . .'
I say to Nigel, 'Nigel . . .'

This continual repetition of simple structures which introduce speech emphasises the dialogue nature of Lesley's story and captures the to-ing and fro-ing of Nigel from Lesley to Gunther – who never speaks to her. The constant repetition of Nigel's name also adds pace. Nigel, except at the close, is a man of few words. He obviously doesn't care for Lesley's concern for her character's motivation, preferring expressions like: 'No sun is favourite' and 'Sun tan lotion is favourite.'

When he does say more, then repetition is used for humorous effect:

> I said, 'On grounds of health?'
> Nigel said, 'No. On grounds of it making continuity a bugger.'

and

> I said, 'It helps my character.'
> He said, 'What would help your character is if you took your bikini top off.'

Elsewhere, the humour is sometimes more crude – as in the contrast between Emily Brontë and 'knockers'. And, at the end, the humour seems to work in two ways. First, linguistically, we have the unexpected contrast between very short sentences and the long sentence which gives Lesley her motivation to strip. But, semantically, we have the rather sad understanding that the nonsense reported back by Nigel convinces Lesley that it's all right for Travis to slip off her bikini bottom. Of course, this naïve trait of Lesley's runs through the whole piece, as she lays claim to her professionalism.

## Activity

The next two extracts are taken from the beginning of Peter Shaffer's *Lettice and Lovage*. The first extract – Scene 1A – features Miss Lettice Douffet, a guide employed to show the public around sixteenth-century Fustian House. She is dutifully reciting a text she has memorised to a bored group of tourists. But in the second extract – Scene 1C – it is several days later and Lettice is lecturing another group of tourists, who are spellbound by her dramatic recital. Compare the two extracts. How does Lettice's language change? What does she add?

# Text: *Lettice and Lovage*

(*Scene 1A. The grand hall of Fustian House. The main feature is an imposing Tudor staircase of oak which descends into the middle of it. A scarlet rope is stretched across the bottom, denying access to the public. Standing nearby is* MISS LETTICE DOUFFET, *the guide appointed to show people round this gloomy old house.*)

The family motto alludes to an incident which occurred on the Feast of Candlemas 1585 upon this actual staircase. On that night Queen Elizabeth the First, making a Royal Progress through her realm, chose to honour with her presence the yeoman merchant John Fustian. To mark the occasion Fustian caused a banquet to be laid here in this hall, and himself stood by the Queen's side at the top of the stairs to escort her down to it. However, as Her Majesty set foot on the first stair she tripped on the hem of her elaborate dress, and would have fallen, had not her host taken hold of her arm and saved her. The Queen being in merry mood immediately called for a sword and dubbed him a Knight of Her Realm.

(*Scene 1C. Several days later.* LETTICE *is lecturing another group of the public.*)

You are looking now at what is indisputedly the most famous staircase in England! . . . *The Staircase of Aggrandisement!* On the night of February the second, 1585 – a brilliant snowy night – John Fustian laid before his Sovereign here in this hall a monumental feast! The tables were piled high with hedgehogs, puffins and coneys! Also herons, peacocks and swans!

Nothing could exceed in diversity or succulence an Elizabethan feast – and on the night we speak of – in this room – a hundred of the liveliest courtiers stood salivating to consume it. (*Increasingly excited by her tale*) Suddenly she appeared – Gloriana herself, the Virgin Queen of England! – in a blaze of diamonds presented to her by the Czar Ivan the Terrible, who had seen a portrait of her in miniature, and lost a little of his icy heart to her chaste looks! Smiling, she set foot upon the first stair, up there! Alas, as she did so –at that precise moment – she slipped and would have plunged headlong down all fifteen polished and bruising steps, had not her host – standing precisely where I stand now, *at the very bottom – leapt in a single bound* the whole height of the staircase to where she stood, and saved her!

(*One or two gasp with amazement.*)

Imagine the scene! Time as if suspended! A hundred be-ribboned guests frozen like Renaissance statues: arms outstretched in powerless gesture! Eyes wide with terror in the flare of torches! . . . And then suddenly John Fustian moves! He, who up to that moment has lived his whole life as a dull and turgid yeoman, breaks the spell! Springs forward – upward – rises like a bird – like feathered Mercury – *soars* in one astounding leap the whole height of these stairs, and at the last possible moment catches her in his loyal arms, raises her high above his head, and rose-cheeked with triumph cries up to her: 'Adored Majesty! Adored and *Endored* Majesty! Fear not! You are safe! – And your hedgehogs await!'

## *Commentary*

Much of what has been added is description. For example, the Queen becomes Sovereign; Gloriana; Virgin Queen of England.

We noted earlier how anaphoric reference is the use of a pronoun referring back to its earlier noun. Reference forward is called **cataphoric reference** and this occurs with the Queen's arrival being signalled with the pronoun 'she' referring us forward to its proper noun 'Gloriana': 'Suddenly *she* appeared – *Gloriana* herself.' Its effect is to set up expectations – which is totally appropriate in this dramatic account. It's like saying: 'And here she is!'

Detailed **noun phrases** add to the depth and exaggeration of the description. For example: 'fifteen polished and bruising steps' where 'steps' is the head noun and 'fifteen polished and bruising' tells us more about them or pre-modifies them. A noun phrase consists of the main or head noun and can have extra description before the head noun or after, or both. As these extra words can be said to 'modify' the head noun then they are referred to as pre- or post-modifiers. Here are some of the noun phrases from the extract:

| *pre-modifiers* | *head noun* | *post-modifiers* |
|---|---|---|
| most famous | staircase | in England |
| brilliant snowy | night | |
| fifteen polished and bruising | steps | |
| | Gloriana | Virgin Queen of England! in a blaze of diamonds presented to her by the Czar Ivan the Terrible |

The banquet also gains exaggerated detail and becomes:

a monumental feast! The tables were piled high with hedgehogs, puffins and coneys! Also herons, peacocks and swans!
Nothing could exceed in diversity or succulence an Elizabethan feast . . . courtiers stood salivating to consume it

But the biggest change concerns 'the yeoman merchant John Fustian'. He is transformed from 'a dull and turgid yeoman' who 'springs forward – upward – rises like a bird – like feathered Mercury – *soars* in one astounding leap the whole height of these stairs' to save his Queen. The figurative language compares Fustian to a bird, to Mercury even. The dramatic, imaginative effect of language like this is also used when describing the inability of the guests to do anything to help: they are 'frozen like Renaissance statues: arms outstretched in powerless gesture'.

The sentence structure also adds to the drama. Each sentence type becomes an exclamation, helping to express emotion much more directly. This adds to the dramatic and exaggerated description of the 'events' of that night. Perhaps the most direct are the short exclamations aimed at heightening the drama: 'Imagine the scene! Time as if suspended!' The whole speech is clearly a dramatic re-enactment and rises to a climax with embedded speech from the noble hero: '"Adored Majesty! Adored and *En*dored Majesty! Fear not! You are safe! – And your hedgehogs await!"'

*Activity*

Now read this account, from Shakespeare's *Hamlet,* given by the Ghost of how he was murdered. What figurative language can you find? And what effect do the examples of repetition have?

**Text: *Hamlet 2***

Sleeping within my orchard,
My custom always of the afternoon,
Upon my secure hour thy uncle stole,
With juice of cursed hebona in a vial,
And in the porches of my ears did pour
The leprous distillment, whose effect
Holds such an enmity with blood of man
That swift as quicksilver it courses through
The natural gates and alleys of the body,
And with a sudden vigor it doth posset
And curd, like eager droppings into milk,
The thin and wholesome blood. So did it mine,
And a most instant tetter bark'd about,
Most lazar-like, with vile and loathsome crust
All my smooth body.
Thus was I, sleeping, by a brother's hand
Of life, of crown, of queen, at once dispatch'd,
Cut off even in the blossoms of my sin,
Unhous'led, disappointed, unanel'd,
No reck'ning made, but sent to my account
With all my imperfections on my head.
O, horrible, O, horrible, most horrible!

## *Commentary*

The Ghost is describing to Hamlet how, whilst he slept, Hamlet's uncle poured the poison hebenon into his ears and this coursed through his veins, curdled his blood and caused his skin to erupt like leprosy ('lazar-like') and become crusted and covered as bark does a tree ('bark'd about'). Furthermore, he was killed before he could make a confession of his sins. 'Unhous'led' refers to the fact that he has been sent to his death before having had the chance to be absolved by a priest – without having taken the sacrament, unprepared and unanointed ('unanel'd') with oil. As such, his soul is still stained with sin and he will have to answer for this on the day of reckoning.

The main use of figurative language is in comparing the natural body to the man-made world of the city. The ears and veins of the body are like the entrances and roads of a city, as if the body was a whole world unto itself. Other comparisons are:

swift as quicksilver
posset/ And curd, like eager droppings into milk
lazar-like
bark'd about

These are effective comparisons to show the speed of change and also suggest the horrific appearance of the skin. The height of the Ghost's sins is suggested by the comparison to a flower still in blossom – again, a natural image; this continues the 'tree' image of the bark-like skin.

The main examples of repetition concern the use of **three part lists**. Giving things in threes is an effective, and often persuasive, way of making a point. Examples are: ABC; ready steady go; government of the people, by the people, for the people. Shakespeare gives the Ghost three examples of three part lists:

Of life, of crown, of queen
Unhous'led, disappointed, unanel'd
O, horrible, O, horrible, most horrible!

The final three part list is effective in its simplicity of repetition: the anguish that the Ghost feels, doomed as it is to walk in the shadowy world of purgatory.

*Extension*

This unit has focused on four quite different kinds of story. Willy's story from *Death of a Salesman* is useful in tracing how Labov's theory of oral narratives might be replicated in a written script. Bennett's monologue relies heavily on embedded speech, and its humour owes much to repetition. The humour in Shaffer's *Lettice and Lovage*, on the other hand, is derived largely from the exaggerated use of figurative language. The final extract from *Hamlet* also draws heavily on imagery as well as using three part lists.

In all cases these stories have structure and cohesion. Without them the stories wouldn't flow or, perhaps, make sense. Extension work could follow up the various features highlighted in this unit, focusing, for example, on Labov's theories, or working out how – linguistically – humour works. *The Language of Humour* by Alison Ross has a section on drama which might be useful here.

1    For specific extension work take a scene involving several characters, then re-write it as a monlogue from one character's point of view – along the lines of Bennett's Lesley in *Her Big Chance*. Alternatively, Caryl Churchill's *Fen* features several characters telling stories and any of these would be fruitful to analyse.
2    Compare these three film openings. Analyse them using Labov's theory of oral narrative and the features of cohesion.

From *Goodfellas*. Henry Hill is speaking:

> as far back as I can remember I always wanted to be a gangster (.) to me being a gangster was better than being president of the United States (.) even before I first wandered into the cab stand for an after-school job I knew that I wanted to be a part of them (.) it was there that I knew that I belonged (.) to me it meant being somebody in a neighbourhood that was full of nobodies (.) I mean they weren't like anybody else (.) they did what they wanted (.) they double-parked in front of a hydrant nobody ever gave them a ticket (.) in the summer when they played cards all night nobody ever called the cops

From *Casino*. Sam Rothstein is speaking:

> when you love someone you've gotta trust them (.) there's no other way (.) you've gotta give them the key to everything that's yours (.) otherwise what's the point (.) and for a while I believed that's the kind of love I had

From *Taxi Driver*. Travis Bichel is speaking:

May tenth (.) thank god for the rain (.) she's helped wash away the garbage and the trash off the sidewalks (.) I'm working long hours now (.) six in the afternoon to six in the morning (.) sometimes even eight in the morning (.) six days a week (.) sometimes even seven days a week (.) it's a long hustle but it keeps me real busy (.) I can take in three (.) three-fifty a week (.) sometimes even more when I do it off the meter (.) all the animals come out at night (.) whores (.) skunk pussies (.) buggers (.) queens (.) fairies (.) dopers (.) junkies (.) sick venal (.)

someday a real rain'll come and wash all the scum off the streets (.) I take people all over (.) I take people to the Bronx (.) Brooklyn (.) I take 'em to Harlem (.) I don't care (.) it don't make no difference to me (.) it does to some (.) some won't even take spooks (.) don't make no difference to me

# The grammar of sound

This unit will build on and extend some of the features previously discussed in Units 4 and 5, particularly the features of cohesion and syntax repetition. The extracts in this unit could be termed 'anti-realistic' in many ways, in that theirs is a language which, perhaps, is more consciously 'poetic' than some of the earlier extracts in this book. The language of the extracts in this unit seem more consciously to strive for patterns and a sense of rhythm. Ultimately they are very conscious of the sound of their language.

*Activity*

Although not obviously 'poetic', this monologue by Miss Scoons on the dream of stardom, from Sam Shepard's *Angel City*, has a pattern, a kind of rhythm. Read it, out loud if possible, and decide what gives it that rhythm.

## Text: *Angel City*

> I look at the screen and I am the screen . . . I look at the movie and I am the movie. I am the star. . . . For days I am the star and I'm not me. I'm me being the star. I look at my life when I come down . . . and I hate my life when I come down. I hate my life not being a movie. I hate my life not being a star. I hate being myself in my life which isn't a movie and never will be. I hate having to eat. Having to work. Having to sleep. Having to go to the bathroom. Having to get from one place to another with no potential. Having to live in this body which isn't a star's body and all the time knowing that stars exist . . .

## Commentary

The repetition of the same words and the same construction – **syntax repetition** – underpins Miss Scoons' whole speech:

> star . . . movie . . . life
> I look
> I am
> I hate
> Having to

Whole sentences are virtually repeated with just one or two key words altered and this also helps to emphasise those particular words and drive home Miss Scoons' feelings:

> I look at the *screen* and I am the *screen* . . . I look at the *movie* and I am the *movie*. . . . I *look* at my life when I come down . . . and I *hate* my life when I come down.

## Rhythm and stress

This repetition helps to create a **rhythm**. Rhythm, from the Greek meaning 'flowing', is often determined by variation in the level of **stress** given to different syllables. In verse this may be quite regular; in prose, as in this extract, it will be varied. Stress helps the flow of language and also reinforces meaning. And if the same stressed words are repeated then we get a coherent pattern of sound and meaning. Some of the key stressed syllables in this extract – in italics – are:

I *look* at the screen and I *am* the screen . . . I *look* at the movie and
I *am* the movie
I *hate* my life . . .
I *hate hav*ing to eat
*Hav*ing to . . . etc.

Try reading the extract again with these stresses in mind. Variation
could be achieved by deciding how much stress to give other syllables.
For instance, which of these choices seem better?

*Hav*ing to work/*Hav*ing to *work*
*Hav*ing to sleep/*Hav*ing to *sleep*

In the end this tight, staccato speech accumulates words and sounds
to produce a short but powerful statement by a wannabe star.

The most common arrangement of stress in English verse is that
of a weak stress followed by a stronger one. This is known as **iambic
stress** and is felt to most closely mirror the rhythms found in natural
speech. Regular examples from Shakespeare are:

ROMEO:   But, *soft!* What *light* through *yon*der *window breaks?*
HORATIO:   But, *look*, the *morn*, in *russ*et *man*tle *clad*.

Of course writing in verse always in the same stress pattern would prove
monotonous, so playwrights, and poets, may vary their underlying
pattern for effect and to vary the pace. Consider:

HAMLET:   To be, or not to be – that is the question.

Regular iambic stress would give us:

HAMLET:   To *be*, or *not* to *be* – that *is* the *ques*tion.

But a natural reading of this line would want to stress: *that* is the
*ques*tion; or possibly: *that is* the *ques*tion.

Consider, then, which syllables you would stress in these lines
(some of which have already been started above):

ROMEO:   But, soft! What light through yonder breaks?
  It is the east, and Juliet is the sun!
HORATIO:   But, look, the morn, in russet mantle clad,
  Walks o'er the dew of yon high eastern hill.
CALIBAN:   Be not afeard, the isle is full of noises,
  Sounds, and sweet airs, that give delight and hurt not.

Foreign learners of English can experience problems with getting stress in the right place. The Spanish waiter Manuel in the British television series *Fawlty Towers* once had problems addressing some joiners who had come to do some work at the hotel. He said to them: 'You are *Orelly* men' as opposed to 'O'*Reilly*'. And some words gain their American flavour because of a different placing of stress, for example: UK pronunciation – *de*bris/US pronunciation – de*bris*.

### Activity

In this next extract, from Beckett's *Waiting for Godot*, just taking a glance at its layout on the page shows its strong patterning – not only in the dialogue itself but also in the stage directions, the silences which help shape the pace and rhythm of the minimal exchanges. The two tramps, Vladimir and Estragon, are bidding farewell to Pozzo. Again, try to read it out loud. Play around with varying the stress you give to different syllables; also vary the pace: rush some lines, ponder others.

## Text: *Waiting for Godot* 1

ESTRAGON:  Then adieu.
POZZO:  Adieu.
VLADIMIR:  Adieu.
POZZO:  Adieu.

(*Silence. No one moves.*)

VLADIMIR:  Adieu.
POZZO:  Adieu.
ESTRAGON:  Adieu.

(*Silence.*)

POZZO:  And thank you.

VLADIMIR:  Thank you.
POZZO:  Not at all.
ESTRAGON:  Yes yes.
POZZO:  No no.
VLADIMIR:  Yes yes.
ESTRAGON:  No no.

(*Silence.*)

POZZO:  I don't seem to be able . . . (*long hesitation*) . . . to depart.
ESTRAGON:  Such is life.

Read this extract – again from *Waiting for Godot*. What patterns are there?
Are you conscious of the sounds of any particular words or letters? And
what different impressions do you get of Vladimir and Estragon?

## Text: *Waiting for Godot 2*

ESTRAGON:  In the meantime let us try
and converse calmly, since we are
incapable of keeping silent.
VLADIMIR:  You're right, we're
inexhaustible.
ESTRAGON:  It's so we won't think.
VLADIMIR:  We have that excuse.
ESTRAGON:  It's so we won't hear.
VLADIMIR:  We have our reasons.
ESTRAGON:  All the dead voices.
VLADIMIR:  They make a noise like wings.
ESTRAGON:  Like leaves.
VLADIMIR:  Like sand.
ESTRAGON:  Like leaves.

(*Silence.*)

VLADIMIR:  They all speak together.
ESTRAGON:  Each one to itself.

(*Silence.*)

VLADIMIR:  Rather they whisper.
ESTRAGON:  They rustle.
VLADIMIR:  They murmur.

ESTRAGON:  They rustle.

(*Silence.*)

VLADIMIR:  What do they say?
ESTRAGON:  They talk about their lives.
VLADIMIR:  To have lived is not enough
for them.
ESTRAGON:  They have to talk about it.
VLADIMIR:  To be dead is not enough for
them.
ESTRAGON:  It is not sufficient.

(*Silence.*)

VLADIMIR:  They make a noise like
feathers.
ESTRAGON:  Like leaves.
VLADIMIR:  Like ashes.
ESTRAGON:  Like leaves.

(*Long silence.*)

VLADIMIR:  Say something!
ESTRAGON:  I'm trying.

(*Long silence.*)

The syntax repetition lays down a pattern and helps establish a rhythm.
Just in the opening lines we find lots of repetition – here in italics:

ESTRAGON:   *It's so we won't* think.
VLADIMIR:   *We have* that excuse.
ESTRAGON:   *It's so we won't* hear.
VLADIMIR:   *We have* our reasons.
ESTRAGON:   All the dead voices.
VLADIMIR:   They make a noise *like wings.*
ESTRAGON:   *Like leaves.*
VLADIMIR:   *Like sand.*
ESTRAGON:   *Like leaves.*

Of equal interest is the emphasis placed on the sound of particular words or letters. First, take the words: 'whisper'; 'rustle'; 'murmur'. These words are onomatopoeic. **Onomatopoeia** in its simplest form means words which sound like the noise they describe. It is the meaning which creates the effect, not solely the sound of the words. Beckett also uses **alliteration**; this is the repetition of the same consonant or consonant sound, normally at the beginning of words or stressed syllables. The clearest example from the extract is the play on the 'l' in:

> like wings
> Like leaves
> Like sand
> Like leaves

and

> like feathers
> Like leaves
> Like ashes
> Like leaves

We are also conscious of the 'r' sound in: 'whisper/rustle/murmur'. And very obvious when reading these lines out loud is the constant use of the 's' sound. Use of the 's' sound is called **sibilance** (from the Greek, meaning 'hissing') and its repetition is, again, a particular kind of alliteration. So we feel a kind of hypnotic rhythm in the run on of words: 'like feathers/like leaves/like ashes/like leaves'. The effect of all these devices is to bind the dialogue into a coherent pattern of sound. Of course what also strengthens the effect is the meaning of the words – which are *about* sound: 'hear/voices/noise/speak/whisper/rustle/ murmur/say/talk'.

The silences are dead and empty. You may have noted that it is Vladimir who initiates conversation; Estragon who kills it. Twice Estragon can only repeat what he has said before. A sensitive reading should reveal the panic of Vladimir trying to say something, 'anything at all!', in order to fill the silences, the void that scares them. As one critic once remarked: 'Vladimir and Estragon are ad-libbing for their very lives.'

*Activity*

These next two extracts are from Shakespeare's *The Tempest*. The two speeches are spoken by Caliban, apparently the beast of the island or 'thou earth' as Prospero calls him. Caliban is talking to his new masters, Stephano and Trinculo. Yet, paradoxically, while they talk in prose, Caliban's words are in verse – a form reserved for more elevated language. What sounds stand out? What impression do his words create?

## Text: *The Tempest* 1

I prithee let me bring thee where crabs grow:
And I with my long nails will dig thee pig-nuts,
Show thee a jay's nest, and instruct thee how
To snare the nimble marmazet. I'll bring thee
To clust'ring filberts, and sometimes I'll get thee
Young scamels from the rock. Wilt thou go with me?

## Text: *The Tempest* 2

Be not afeard, the isle is full of noises,
Sounds, and sweet airs, that give delight and hurt not.
Sometimes a thousand twangling instruments
Will hum about mine ears; and sometime voices,
That if I then had wak'd after long sleep,
Will make me sleep again, and then in dreaming,
The clouds methought would open, and show riches
Ready to drop upon me, that when I wak'd
I cried to dream again.

75

## *Commentary*

Despite Caliban's claims earlier in the play that the main advantage of being taught language by Prospero is that he now knows how to curse, these two speeches are meant to show clearly his knowledge and understanding of the island as well as his wonder at and appreciation of some of its magical qualities. The first text reveals his almost childlike eagerness to show Stephano and Trinculo some of the hidden edible delights available to those who know where to look. He says:

> (I'll) dig thee
> show thee
> instruct thee
> bring thee
> get thee

ending with the honest and open invitation: 'Wilt thou go with me?' The items of food themselves sound delicious; there is much use of alliteration and sibilance which enriches the meanings of the words. The sounds which most stand out, perhaps, are the 'g', 'm', 'l', 'r' and of course the 's':

> crabs grow
> dig thee pig-nuts
> nimble marmazet
> clust'ring filberts
> scamels from the rock

And also perhaps for the modern reader, the fact that we may not be sure what some of these food items exactly are may further enhance their appeal. We can let the sounds of the words do their work without worrying about the connotations certain foods may have for us. Caliban is actually referring to: crab apples, peanuts, marmosets (small monkeys) and hazelnuts. There are different opinions as to what scamels are meant to be; these range from wading snipes to some type of shellfish.

Caliban's second speech is more onomatopoeic and, indeed, much of it is concerned with sweet sounds and music. There are words like: 'twangling' and 'hum'; and generally sibilance runs through the extract, connecting the ideas in a cohesive pattern of sound. The overall effect could be described as a good example of **euphony**. Euphony (from the Greek, meaning 'well sounding') refers to language which has a pleasing, smooth and musical effect; the opposite – clashing, ugly sounds – is cacophony. Overall, then, this rich and harmonious-sounding language gives Caliban an eloquence and grandeur which apparently contradicts his menial status.

Juliet's words as she finds Romeo dead and decides to take her own life give an example of **assonance**. Assonance is the vowel equivalent of alliteration. We can note in these few lines the 'o' and 'u' sounds and particularly the 'i' sound in: 'I will kiss thy lips'.

What's here? A cup clos'd in my true love's hand?
Poison, I see, hath been his timeless end.
O churl, drunk all, and left no friendly drop
To help me after? I will kiss thy lips,
Haply some poison yet doth hang on them,
To make me die with a restorative. (*Kisses him*)
Thy lips are warm.

*Activity*

The next text is set in the County Donegal of 1936. This speech by Michael, who acts as narrator of the story, concludes Brian Friel's *Dancing at Lughnasa* (1990). The richly evocative words illustrate the sound features discussed above, but they also serve as a good example of the cohesive links discussed in Unit 5. A careful reading, particularly out loud, should also reveal its underlying rhythms and reflective tone. Read it and analyse it with these thoughts in mind. Often, with longer extracts, it's a good idea to first get a sense of what the extract is about and, then, look at how it's expressed – the words and the syntax.

## Text: *Dancing at Lughnasa*

And so, when I cast my mind back to that summer of 1936, different kinds of memories offer themselves to me.

But there is one memory of that Lughnasa time that visits me most often; and what fascinates me about that memory is that it owes nothing to fact. In that memory atmosphere is more real than incident and everything is simultaneously actual and illusory. In that memory, too, the air is nostalgic with the music of the thirties. It drifts in from somewhere far away – a mirage of sound – a dream music that is both heard and imagined; that seems to be both itself and its own echo; a sound so alluring and so mesmeric that the afternoon is bewitched, maybe haunted, by it. And what is so strange about that memory is that everybody seems to be floating on those sweet sounds, moving rhythmically, languorously, in complete isolation; responding more to the mood of the music than to its beat. When I remember it, I think of it as dancing. Dancing with eyes half closed because to open them would break the spell. Dancing as if language had surrendered to movement – as if this ritual, this wordless ceremony, was now the way to speak, to whisper private and sacred things, to be in touch with some otherness. Dancing as if the very heart of life and all its hopes might be found in those assuaging notes and those hushed rhythms and in those silent and hypnotic movements. Dancing as if language no longer existed because words were no longer necessary.

## Commentary

The narrator is trying to express his remembrances of the summer of 1936 and in so doing is trying to articulate the nature and feel of memory; memory as an idea and actual memory of those former times. In the end he comes up with the idea that the only way to express those memories is through the notion of dancing. And of course he's using words to express these ideas but also deciding that words are inadequate to describe what he wants; in the end he can only think using the language and idea of dancing.

The extract draws on words from the semantic field of sound and music; 'memory' and 'dancing' are continually repeated. Perhaps, though, what stands out most markedly are words to do with dreams, magic or mystery. Added to this there are onomatopoeic words which help to create the sense and sound of dream-like music. We could produce the following list:

| words to do with reality | unreality | onomatopoeic words |
|---|---|---|
| fact | illusory | rhythmically |
| real | mirage | languorously |
| actual | dream | whisper |
| | imagined | assuaging notes |
| | alluring | hushed rhythms |
| | mesmeric | |
| | bewitched | |
| | haunted | |
| | strange | |
| | spell | |
| | ritual | |
| | ceremony | |
| | sacred | |
| | otherness | |
| | hypnotic | |

As noted earlier in this unit, the simplest form of onomatopoeia concerns words which sound like the noise they describe. However, in its widest sense we can also label onomatopoeic words whose sounds somehow seem to give an impression which reinforces their meaning. To this wider definition we could, therefore, add the words: 'mirage/mesmeric/bewitched/haunted'. These words, arguably, add to the overall magical mystery of the piece.

Finally, the long sentence structures, the cohesive links and the syntax repetition also help to create the reflective, lyrical atmosphere of the extract.

The opening obviously sets the scene for a thoughtful reflection on what was: 'And so, when I cast my mind back . . .'. The words from the semantic field of unreality form links because of their similar meanings. These virtual synonyms heap up on each other to emphasise the 'otherness' of the memories for Michael of 1936 County Donegal. There are many linking structures, particularly at the beginning of sentences, but also throughout. To take just one example:

> *It* drifts in from somewhere far away – a mirage of sound – a dream music *that is both* heard and imagined; *that seems to be both* itself and its own echo; a sound *so* alluring *and so* mesmeric that the afternoon is bewitched, maybe haunted, by *it*.

Our focus here is on the words which structure the sentence – here in italics; the important cohesion of words with real 'meaning' such as 'mirage/ dream', etc. has already been noted. The first word of the sentence links back to 'memory', mentioned in all the preceding sentences – an example of anaphoric reference. The last word of our highlighted sentence also echoes the first. The other italicised words also echo each other and bring an ordered balance, giving the impression of a thoughtful, reflective speech.

Towards the end of Michael's speech the word (and idea) of 'dancing' clearly stands out; this starts off each new thought and sentence:

Dancing with eyes half closed
Dancing as if language
Dancing as if the very heart
Dancing as if language

All these links help to create the underlying rhythm and, certainly, the important words will be stressed. Friel's extract is a nice contrast to Shepard's monologue which opened this unit. There the stresses went hand in hand with a shorter, blunter sentence structure. Friel's longer sentences yield a lyrical and evocative tone, dance-like in its rhythm and totally appropriate for its subject matter.

### Extension

1    The rest of Brian Friel's *Dancing at Lughnasa* is worth exploring, particularly other speeches by Michael or tales from Africa delivered by his Uncle Jack. Here is part of Jack's description of a Ugandan festival:

We light fires round the periphery of the circle; and we paint our faces with coloured powders; and we sing local songs; and we drink palm wine. And then we dance – and dance – and dance – children, men, women, most of them lepers, many of them with misshapen limbs, with missing limbs – dancing, believe it or not, for days on end!

2    Analyse one of Sam Shepard's monologues. This is Shooter, from *Action*, speaking of the risks and necessities of acting:

You go outside. The world's quiet. White. Everything resounding. Not a sound of a motor. Not a light. You see into the house. You see the candles. You watch the people. You can see what it's like inside. The candles draw you. You get a cold feeling being outside. Separated. You have an idea that being inside it's cosier. Friendlier. Warmth. People. Conversation. Everyone using a language. Then you go inside. It's a shock. It's not like how you expected. You lose what you had outside. You forget that there even is an outside. The inside is all you know. You hunt for a way of being with everyone. A way of finding how to behave. You find out what's expected of you. You act yourself out.

# Book to film

The writer Ian McEwan describes his approach to producing a screenplay of Timothy Mo's novel *Sour Sweet* as that of the hooligan builder demolishing a mansion built with loving care. 'By the time I am finished,' he writes, 'this house will be a roofless shack.' And of the characters living in that mansion he says: 'Each of these people comes with a history, a little biography, a past that seems really to have been lived. When I am through with them, these jokers will have nothing to show but what they say or do, and there won't be much of that.'

The ten hours or so that it might take to read a full-length novel is reduced to 100 minutes of screen time. The screenplay has more in common with the short story: it must establish characters and situations with speed, take their world as granted and cannot risk off-plot indulgences or frayed ends. Everything must count. Of course, most film audiences are sophisticated ones; they 'read' the signs – the images, sounds, references – just as sensitive readers read novels. In that way, setting, mood and character can be quickly established.

## Activity

This screenplay (on page 83) is by Emma Thompson and is adapted from Jane Austen's novel *Sense and Sensibility* (below). In this extract Marianne Dashwood, having fallen and injured her ankle, is rescued by Willoughby. Compare the two extracts. How has Emma Thompson made the incident more dramatic? What impressions are conveyed of Willoughby's character and how are they conveyed?

# Text: Jane Austen's *Sense and Sensibility*

A gentleman carrying a gun, with two pointers playing around him, was passing up the hill and within a few yards of Marianne when her accident happened. He put down his gun and ran to her assistance. She had raised herself from the ground, but her foot had been twisted in the fall, and she was scarcely able to stand. The gentleman offered his services, and perceiving that her modesty declined what her situation rendered necessary, took her up without farther delay and carried her down the hill. Then passing through the garden, the gate of which had been left open by Margaret, he bore her directly into the house, whither Margaret was just arrived, and quitted not his hold till he had seated her in a chair in the parlour.

Elinor and her mother rose up in amazement at their entrance, and while the eyes of both were fixed on him with an evident wonder and a secret admiration which equally sprung from his appearance, he apologised for his intrusion by relating its cause, in a manner so frank and so graceful that his person, which was uncommonly handsome, received additional charms from his voice and expression. Had he been even old, ugly, and vulgar, the gratitude and kindness of Mrs Dashwood would have been secured by any act of attention to her child; but the influence of youth, beauty and elegance gave an interest to the action which came home to her feelings.

She thanked him again and again, and with a sweetness of address which always attended her invited him to be seated. But this he declined, as he was dirty and wet. Mrs Dashwood then begged to know to whom she was obliged. His name, he replied, was Willoughby, and his present home was at Allenham, from whence he hoped she would allow him the honour of calling tomorrow to inquire after Miss Dashwood. The honour was readily granted, and he then departed, to make himself still more interesting, in the midst of an heavy rain.

# Text: Emma Thompson's *Sense and Sensibility*

(MARIANNE *tries to get up, but the pain in her ankle is too great. She sinks back to the ground.* MARGARET *is very alarmed.*)

MARIANNE:   Margaret, run home and fetch help.

(*The mists have thickened. They can no longer see where they are. Despite her rising fear,* MARGARET *squares her shoulders bravely and tries to sense the direction.*)

MARGARET:   I think it is this way. I will run as fast as I can, Marianne.

(*She dashes off. As she goes into the mist we hear the thunder of hooves. CU Margaret's terrified expression. They seem to be coming from all around. She wheels and turns and then – Crash! Through the mist breaks a huge white horse. Astride sits an Adonis in hunting gear.* MARGARET *squeals. The horse rears. Its rider controls it and slides off. He rushes to* MARIANNE's *side.*)

THE STRANGER:   Are you hurt?
MARIANNE (*transfixed*):   Only my ankle.
THE STRANGER:   May I have your permission to—

(*He indicates her leg. Decorous, perhaps faintly impish.*)

THE STRANGER:   —ascertain if there are any breaks?

(MARIANNE *nods speechlessly. With great delicacy, he feels her ankle.* MARGARET's *eyes are out on chapel-hooks.* MARIANNE *almost swoons with embarrassment and excitement mixed.*)

THE STRANGER:   It is not broken. Now, can you put your arm about my neck?

(MARIANNE *does not need any encouragement. He lifts her effortlessly and calls to his horse: 'Bedivere!' It trots obediently forward. The* STRANGER *smiles down at* MARIANNE.)

THE STRANGER:   Allow me to escort you home.

(INT. BARTON COTTAGE. DINING ROOM. DAY.)

(*Rain is thudding against the window from which* MRS DASHWOOD *turns, looking very worried.*)

MRS DASHWOOD:   Marianne was sure it would not rain.
ELINOR:   Which invariably means it will.

(*But we can see she is trying to conceal her anxiety from her mother. There are noises in the hall.*)

MRS DASHWOOD:   At last!

(MARGARET *runs into the room dripping wet.*)

MARGARET:   She fell over! She fell down – and he's carrying her!

(INT. BARTON COTTAGE. FRONT DOOR. DAY.)

(MRS DASHWOOD *and* ELINOR *rush to the front door. They see the* STRANGER *carrying* MARIANNE *up the garden path, his scarlet coat staining the monochrome rain.*)

MRS DASHWOOD: Marianne!

(*The* STRANGER *reaches the door. This is no time for introductions.*)

ELINOR: In here, sir – this way. Margaret, open the door wider. Please, sir, lay her here. Marianne, are you in pain?

(*They move into the parlour.*)

(INT. BARTON COTTAGE. PARLOUR. DAY.)

(MARIANNE *is carried in, surrounded by* ELINOR, MRS DASHWOOD *and* MARGARET.)

THE STRANGER: It is a twisted ankle.
MARIANNE: Do not be alarmed, Mamma.

(*The* STRANGER *deposits* MARIANNE *on the sofa. They look straight into each other's eyes. Electric.*)

THE STRANGER: I can assure you it is not serious. I took the liberty of feeling the bone and it is perfectly sound.

(ELINOR *raises her eyebrows at* MARIANNE, *who blushes to her roots.*)

MRS DASHWOOD: Sir, I cannot even begin to thank you.
THE STRANGER: Please do not think of it. I am honoured to be of service.
MRS DASHWOOD: Will you not be seated?

THE STRANGER: Pray excuse me – I have no desire to leave a water mark! But permit me to call tomorrow afternoon and enquire after the patient?
MRS DASHWOOD: We shall look forward to it!

(*He turns to* MARIANNE *and smiles. She smiles back gloriously. He bows, and sweeps out of the room.*)

MARIANNE (*hissing*): His name! His name!

(MRS DASHWOOD *silences her with a gesture and follows him out with all the solicitous charm she can command while* MARGARET *pokes her head around the door to watch.* ELINOR *is removing* MARIANNE's *boot and trying not to laugh at her.*)

(EXT. BARTON COTTAGE. FRONT DOOR DAY. DAY.)

(MRS DASHWOOD *calls out after him.*)

MRS DASHWOOD: Please tell us to whom we are so much obliged?

(*The* STRANGER *mounts Bedivere and turns to her.*)

THE STRANGER: John Willoughby of Allenham – your servant, ma'am!

(*And he gallops off into the mist – we almost expect Bedivere to sprout wings.*)

## Commentary

In Jane Austen's original prose Willoughby – first referred to as the 'gentleman' – is passing near the stricken Marianne. He picks her up, carries her home, then departs in the rain. What he exactly says Austen doesn't tell us but his manner is 'frank and graceful'.

Emma Thompson's screenplay does supply the dialogue, as well as informative screenplay directions. Willoughby – referred to as the more dashing-sounding 'stranger' – appears out of nowhere, on his horse, looking like a god to save the day. His dramatic entrance is seen through the frightened eyes of Marianne's younger sister Margaret: '*She dashes off. As she goes into the mist we hear the thunder of hooves. CU Margaret's terrified expression.*' His exit is equally dramatic. He sweeps out of the room before announcing his name and gallops off into the mist; Thompson adds wryly that '*we almost expect Bedivere to sprout wings*'.

The suggestive nature of the relationship between Marianne and Willoughby is played up: he '*impishly*' asks if he may touch her leg; a shot of Margaret is used to comment on this – her '*eyes are out on chapel-hooks*'. Later, as he lays her on the sofa, they '*look straight into each other's eyes. Electric*', and a shot of the older sister, Elinor, as she '*raises her eyebrows*' reinforces the moment. Margaret's general excitement and Mrs Dashwood's concern add to the drama.

Willoughby turns out to be an unreliable suitor; perhaps from Thompson's screenplay we do get the impression that he's almost too good to be true. Marianne's eventual husband – most Austen heroines eventually get the man they deserve – is the older but more reliable Colonel Brandon. Cleverly Thompson completely invents a parallel scene later on as Brandon finds and carries a rain-drenched Marianne to warmth and safety after she had wandered far from home.

## What? No narrator?

Often a core problem for the screenwriter is to present events without explaining them. The novelist can, and often does, narrate. They can present events and easily comment on them – either openly or through the thoughts of their characters. With some notable exceptions, films rarely work with narrators (see the extracts at the end of Unit 5). Ian McEwan, working to preserve some of the warmth of Timothy Mo's narration in *Sour Sweet* as well as the humour in many of the situations, became aware in his various drafts for his screenplay that the film was floating free of the novel.

## *Activity*

Compare these two extracts – the first from Mo's novel, the second from McEwan's script. In this incident Grandpa, who has come over to London from Hong Kong to settle with his family, has invited English friends round for 'tea'. A tea which consists of mince, jam tart and custard. Much of the novel revolves around amusing misconceptions between Chinese and English views of life. These are normally conveyed through the author's narrative stance and, without a narrator, many were abandoned in the film. But this extract survived. Compare the two versions. How does McEwan present the events rather than explain them?

# Text: *Timothy Mo's Sour Sweet*

'Speak for foreign devil friends to hear we go outside now,' he told Mui. 'Have something to show old people to make them happy.' Grandpa hopped out spryly, in his enthusiasm without a stick, while Mui marshalled the elderly folk (no mean task) for their breath of fresh air.

Grandpa had just thrown a tarpaulin over whatever it was he had to show as Mui ushered his guests into the yard. Contrary to what Lily had earlier supposed, there were muttered complaints amongst the old people about being turned out into the open, especially at such short notice. Lily brought up the rear, shepherding two or three elderly malcontents who clutched their shawls or jackets meaningfully. She was gentle but firm with them. 'You go into garden, old people. Good and nice thing to see.' She was supporting the nodding old lady with the stick, more or less carrying her tiny weight in fact, while the old person cast bewildered, frightened looks around her with the big watery blue eyes of her race and age.

Grandpa was limping up and down, just about beside himself with glee, in front of three rows of murmuring people. Lily urged forward the old folk at the sides so that they made a rough semi-circle, a friendlier and more informal configuration. 'Ready, Grandpa,' she called.

Grandpa stepped forward. With as much of a flourish as his arthritic shoulder permitted him, he whipped off the tarpaulin. Lily blinked. She knew the shape of what she was looking at; it just took a moment to absorb and digest its significance. Propped against the wall at a 45 degree angle were a coffin and coffin-lid in smoothed but unvarnished wood.

Mui sucked in her breath. There were three seconds of silence before a swelling murmur of angry protest arose from the onlookers.

The old lady Lily was supporting plucked at her sleeve. 'What is it? What is it?' she demanded agitatedly, at last showing some interest in what was going on around her. Grandpa, beaming, oblivious to even the possibility of unfavourable reaction, wrung his gnarled carpenter's hands, bowing his head into hunched shoulders. Taking the grace-saying old gentleman by the arm, he dragged him forward. Grandpa pointed to him, then to the coffin, indicating it was long enough to accommodate his English height and trying to get him to step in and try it out for size.

The old gentleman pulled away, beating at Grandpa's hand. He backed off, banging into others in the row behind who were already trying to squeeze through the kitchen door all at once.

'Don't be shy!' Grandpa called. 'Don't fear. I'm making one for all of you. Not dear at all.' He tried to seize another retreating old gentleman who beat him off. 'Tell them, Mui.'

Lily's old lady, now able to see the coffin, began to sing in her trembling voice 'Abide with me'.

Mui forced her way against the general direction to the front and was scolding Grandpa. He brushed her aside, still with a big beam on his face, and tried to capture another fleeing pensioner. Instead he found Mr Constantinides who, presented with the exhibits by proud Grandpa, said something strange but appropriate-sounding like 'Far kin aid her.'

# Text: Ian McEwan's *Sour Sweet*

GRANDPA: Tell my English friends it's time to go out into garden now. I've got something to show them.

LILY: What is it? You can tell me now.

(*But* GRANDPA *smiles and turns away.*)

(*Cut to:*)
(*Moments later.* LILY *and* MUI *are ushering the old folk out of the room towards the back garden.* LILY *is helping an old lady with a stick towards the door.*)

LILY: Come into garden, please. Something very special for you to look at.

(*Cut to:*)
(*The garden. The thing* GRANDPA *has been constructing is large and leans against the wall. It is covered with sacks. He limps up and down beside it waiting for the last of the old people to come into the yard.* GRANDPA *wants to make a speech.* MUI *stands at his side and acts as translator. He mutters his lines into her ears, she calls out hers to the crowd.*)

GRANDPA: Say welcome to my foreign devil friends.

MUI: Honourable friends, welcome!

(*There is applause.*)

GRANDPA: Say, they are not here to eat food and drink tea and use the toilet, but for a very important purpose.

MUI: Ah . . . we hope you enjoyed the banquet.

(*There is a murmur of assent.*)

GRANDPA: Say, we are all very, very old, weak people who will not live much longer.

MUI: And . . . we wish you long life!

(*More applause.*)

GRANDPA: Some of us might die tomorrow . . .

MUI: Ah . . . *very* long life.

GRANDPA: Tell them, it's time to start making arrangements for death.

MUI: Grandpa! . . . We hope you all come again soon.

GRANDPA: Tell them, I am a carpenter. I have built something they will all be needing . . .

(GRANDPA, *with a self-important flourish, pulls the sacks away.* MUI *has her back to him and continues to translate in a stunned silence.*)

MUI: Grandpa is a carpenter and he has made something specially for all of you . . . and hopes it will be useful . . .

(MUI *turns.* LILY *covers her face with her hands. Propped against the wall is a coffin and coffin lid in smooth unvarnished wood. Undeterred,* GRANDPA *continues his speech into* MUI's *ear.*)

GRANDPA: Tell them, it's very good wood, very good wood . . .

(*There is a gathering hum of protest, anger, fear.* GRANDPA *goes forward and takes the sleeve of an old man in the front row. He tries to entice him nearer the coffin, pointing at the man and then at the coffin to indicate an appropriate fit. He's grinning encouragingly. The flock is edging away, and now is moving as one towards the house.* GRANDPA *continues to pluck at sleeves, trying to pull some of the other old people towards the coffin.*)

Don't be shy . . . don't be shy.

(*The old lady whom* LILY *helped starts to sing 'Abide with me'. There is now a general move towards the house.* GRANDPA *stands by his coffin, genuinely astonished that no one is taking up his offer.*)

## Commentary

McEwan cleverly manages to retain the humour in the scene by the invention of Mui 'translating' Grandpa's words. In fact this screenplay version is arguably more amusing. The understanding, or misunderstanding, of Western life and attitudes through Chinese eyes is presented and reinforced through the mismatch of what Grandpa wants to say and what, in fact, Mui delivers. Mui has managed to bridge the cultures of East and West and her discomfiture at having to replace Grandpa's obviously inappropriate words with something more welcome to the old English people neatly demonstrates this. She has to pause and think quickly before 'translating'. Some of the most amusing changes of meaning concern Grandpa's talk of impending death which Mui renders into prayers for long life.

Much of the action of Mo's original is retained: Grandpa waiting impatiently to show off his creation, his artistic flourish as he removes the tarpaulin cover, his dragging of the old man towards the coffin, the behaviour of the old people. Even the darkly comic moment as the old lady starts to sing 'Abide with me' fits suitably into the new dramatic version. The original extract, though, ends with an authorial viewpoint which the medium of film cannot easily present. Mr Constantinides' comment on the proceedings is obviously 'Fucking Ada' but we hear this through Grandpa's ears as 'Far kin aid her' which Grandpa naturally finds strange but thinks is appropriate.

McEwan's own comment on this scene is interesting. In the process of adapting *Sour Sweet* for the screen he says that numerous changes were made to the order of scenes for reasons he has now forgotten and, in fact, there came a time when he could no longer distinguish between the original and the screenplay. When he took Timothy Mo to see the set during filming and he praised the scene above, McEwan says he was astonished for he was certain Mo had written it that way himself.

## Extension

1    Consider other adaptations of Jane Austen novels. You could compare various versions of *Pride and Prejudice* – either film or BBC versions. How has the language changed over time?

You might like to script scenes where Austen provides no dialogue. Invariably when the hero proposes to the heroine she doesn't tell us what they say. Try writing the screenplay for this scene at the end of *Sense and Sensibility* when Edward Ferrars (played by

Hugh Grant in Emma Thompson's film) proposes to Elinor (played by Emma Thompson):

> His errand at Barton, in fact, was a simple one. It was only to ask Elinor to marry him; and considering that he was not altogether inexperienced in such a question, it might be strange that he should feel so uncomfortable in the present case as he really did, so much in need of encouragement and fresh air.
>
> How soon he had walked himself into the proper resolution, however, how soon an opportunity of exercising it occurred, in what manner he expressed himself, and how he was received, need not be particularly told. This only need be said: – that when they all sat down to table at four o'clock, about three hours after his arrival, he had secured his lady, engaged her mother's consent, and was not only in the rapturous profession of the lover, but in the reality of reason and truth, one of the happiest of men.

Now, compare your script with Thompson's version.

2    Comparisons of Thomas Hardy's and Charles Dickens' novels with their screen adaptations can also be fruitful. Dickens' screenplays, in particular, are continually being re-written – again for film or television. *Bleak House*, *David Copperfield*, *Oliver Twist* and *Great Expectations* are popular choices, the latter, like *Emma*, having been re-located to modern day USA in one version.

3    Finally, consider adaptations of Raymond Chandler novels, particularly *The Big Sleep*. The first version, released in 1946, starred Humphrey Bogart as the private investigator Philip Marlowe. In this first adaptation large chunks of the novel's original text went unchanged into the screenplay. Perhaps not surprisingly, Chandler was said to be very impressed. Chandler's 'hard-boiled' dialogue would make a useful comparison with Quentin Tarantino's work.

# index of terms

This is a form of combined glossary and index. Listed below are some of the main key terms used in the book, together with brief definitions for purposes of reference. The page references will normally take you to the first use of the term in the book, where it is shown in bold.

**accent**  22
> The pronunciation of words.

**adjacency pairs**  22
> The minimal response needed for a dialogue to take place produces a two-way exchange. Two of the most common are:

> greeting–greeting
> question–question.

For example:

A:  good morning
B:  morning

Sometimes exchanges are not immediately followed up and other dialogue takes place before the second half of the pair is produced. This is called an **insertion sequence** as in:

A:  what's your age
B:  what's yours
A:  18
A:  so am I

Here we have a question–answer adjacency pair embedded inside another question and answer pair. If the dialogue wanders off onto what appears to be a complete side issue before coming back to the required second response, then these are called **side sequences**.

**alliteration**  74
> The repetition of the same consonant or consonant sound, normally at the beginning of words or stressed syllables.

**anaphoric reference**  59
> A cohesive link referring back to something already mentioned in a text. For example: 'My father's flying back to the UK today but his Alitalia flight is delayed three hours.' The main link back is 'his' to 'father' but there's also a link back between 'flight' and 'flying'. (See also **cohesion** and **cataphoric reference**.)

**antagonist**  50
> The opponent to the protagonist.

**assonance**  77
> The vowel equivalent of **alliteration**, that is, the repetition of vowel sounds in words close to each other.

**base form**  38
> The starting point for all verbs. Think of it as the infinitive without the 'to' part. For example: eat; have.

**cataphoric reference**  64
> A cohesive feature, this is a reference forward to something coming in the text. For example: 'This is the position. You'll miss your connection in Milan so will have to stay there overnight.' Here the first

sentence points forward to its explanation. (See also **cohesion** and **anaphoric reference**.)

**catharsis** 6

Catharsis is the Aristotelian concept whereby our strong emotions are purged away by seeing their representation on stage.

**cohesion** 58

The features that link texts together. They can function within a sentence and across or between sentences. **Lexical cohesion** concerns links in the meanings or semantics of words. Direct repetition and synonym repetition are the two most common examples. We can also distinguish another form of cohesion, less concerned with meanings of words and more concerned with shaping or joining sentences; this is **grammatical cohesion**. The three most important features concern the use of conjunctions, syntax repetition and pronoun reference. See in particular Willy Loman's speech in Unit 5. **Repetition** (both **direct** and **syntax**) is another important cohesive feature which links and patterns texts. (See also **anaphoric** and **cataphoric reference**.)

**completion points** 28

Completion points are natural ends of statements, or ends of questions, or tag questions (literally questions tagged on to the end of statements). A pause at the completion point naturally gives space for another to start.

**contrasting pair** 49

This is where the second half of an utterance mirrors and neatly balances the first. For example: tough on crime; tough on the causes of crime (political election slogan).

**co-operative principle** 28

Some of the unwritten rules which underpin and enable conversation to work. Formulated by Paul Grice, these rules state that we interpret language on the assumption that speakers are obeying the four maxims of:

1 *quality* (being true)
2 *quantity* (being brief)
3 *relation* (being relevant)
4 *manner* (being clear).

**dialect** 22, 34

Variations in language concerned with choices and use of words. It's useful to consider dialect in two different ways: its lexis and its grammar. **Lexis** is simply the choice of particular words when dealing with semantics or meanings. For example, choices between using: 'ginnel/snicket/alley'.

The **grammar** of a dialect, on the other hand, concerns its way of expressing itself, its syntax or order of words, perhaps. It might also concern its choice of verb forms or its use of the definite article. Examples might be the habit of using tag questions like: 'I missed the bus, didn't I?' which is a grammatical feature of the London dialect.

**direct repetition** 47

Repetition of exactly the same word or words.

**embedded speech** 61

The quoting of dialogue within a story.

**euphony** 76

Euphony (from the Greek, meaning 'well sounding') refers to language which has a pleasing, smooth and musical effect.

**exposition** 12

Setting out the parameters of the drama, giving the audience some idea of what to expect, and perhaps mentioning or introducing the main characters. The opening of *Hamlet* has a clear exposition when the soldiers and Horatio discuss the troubled events in Denmark, talk about the Ghost and introduce young Hamlet into their dialogue.

**eye dialect** 22

Spelling words in such a way so as to indicate how they should be pronounced. For example, (from Edward Bond's *Saved*):

PAM: Yer ain' arf nosey.

**grammar** 35
(see **dialect**)

**grammatical cohesion** 58
(see **cohesion**)

**hedges** 58

Words and phrases which soften or weaken the force with which something is said. Examples of hedges are: 'kind of', 'sort of'. Also words to get the listener to share the speaker's opinion. For example: 'You see what I mean?'.

**iambic stress** 71
(see **rhythm**)

**idiolect** 34

A person's individual language system: their unique pronunciation, grammatical forms and choice of vocabulary.

**insertion sequence** 23
(see **adjacency pairs**)

**kitchen sink drama** 20

Drama of the 1950s which moved from the drawing room environment to the more 'lived-in' settings, sometimes even the kitchen, hence 'kitchen sink'. The issues and language would be appropriately more working class.

**lexical cohesion** 58
(see **cohesion**)

**lexis** 34
(see **dialect**)

**metaphor** 46

Metaphor (from the Greek, meaning 'a carrying over') takes comparison to its logical conclusion by saying that one thing *is* another.

**naturalism** 19

Often used interchangeably with **realism**, its beginnings are associated with the social drama of Ibsen, where the sets, costume and acting were presented as naturalistically as possible.

**noun phrase** 64

A group of words which describe a noun. In the noun phrase above, 'the social drama of Ibsen', the core noun 'drama' is pre-modified with the word 'social' and post-modified with the words 'of Ibsen'.

**onomatopoeia** 74

Words which sound like the noise they describe.

**plant** 61

When an idea or subject is introduced early on, then to be returned to later.

**protagonist** 43

Typically the main character in the drama. See Unit 4.

**realism** 19

Often used interchangeably with **naturalism**. Originally coined to describe drama which developed from naturalism and dealt with riskier issues in a more vigorous way. Used throughout this book to describe drama which deals with everyday issues in a way that is seen as true-to-life. See particularly Unit 2.

**rhetorical question** 49

This is a question that really needs no answer.

**rhythm** 70

This is often determined by variation in the level of stress given to different syllables and helps a text to flow. Different stresses, too, help to give emphasis to significant words. The most common arrangement of stress in English verse is that of a weak stress followed by a stronger one. This is known as **iambic stress** and is felt to most closely mirror the rhythms found in natural speech. For example:

ROMEO: But, *soft*! What *light* through *yon*der *wind*ow *breaks*?

**semantic field** 47

Drawing on words of similar meaning or from the same area of meaning. The semantic field of flying, for example, may encompass such terms as: wing, airport, check-in, baggage allowance.

**sibilance** 74

Use of the 's' sound; its repetition is a particular kind of alliteration.

**side sequence** 23
(see **adjacency pairs**)

**soaps** 28

Arguably, the logical home of realistic theatre – so-called because this kind of programme was originally sponsored by soap manufacturers. They share a much more ephemeral nature than theatre drama: a kind of 'throw-away drama', writers produce hours of new material each week.

**soliloquy** 44

A speech spoken solo allowing the audience to eavesdrop on a character's thoughts.

**Standard English** 22, 37

The prestige variety of English which is used in written forms and in institutional contexts such as government, the law and education.

**stress** 70
(see **rhythm**)

**syntax repetition** 70

Repeating similar strings of words or grammatical structures. An important cohesive feature. For example: 'I look at the screen and I am the screen . . . I look at the movie and I am the movie.'

**tag question** 28

Tags are strings of words which are normally added to a declarative statement and which turn the statement into a question. For example: 'It's cold, isn't it?'

**tail** 37

Added at the end of a statement to give emphasis and orientation. For example: 'It's a knock-out, Hong Kong.'

**three part exchanges** 24

This is where the original speaker follows up the response of the second speaker with some kind of comment or acknowledgement of that response. For example (from Edward Bond's *Saved*):

LEN: Live on yer tod?
PAM: No.
LEN: O.

**three part lists**  66
Giving things in threes is an effective, and often persuasive, way of making a point. For example: government of the people, by the people, for the people.

# index of texts and writers

# references
# and further
# reading

Banks, R.A. and P. Marson (1998) *Drama and Theatre Arts*, London:
    Hodder & Stoughton
Boal, Augusto (1995) *The Rainbow of Desire* (trans. Jackson), London:
    Routledge
Carter, Ronald, Angela Goddard, Danuta Reah, Keith Sanger and Maggie
    Bowring, (1998) *Working with Texts: A core book for language
    analysis*, London: Routledge
Culpeper, Jonathan, Mick Short and Peter Verdonk, (eds) (1998)
    *Exploring the Language of Drama: From Text to Context*, London:
    Routledge
Freeborn, Dennis, Peter French and David Langford (1993) *Varieties of
    English*, 2nd edn, Basingstoke: Macmillan
Grice, Paul (1975) 'Logic and conversation', in Cole, P. and Morgan, J.
    (eds) *Syntax and Semantics*, vol. 3: *Speech Acts*, New York:
    Academic Press
Herman, Vimala (1995) *Dramatic Discourse: Dialogue as Interaction in
    Plays*, London: Routledge
Hiney, Tom (1997) *Raymond Chandler: A Biography*, London: Chatto &
    Windus
Labov, William (1972) 'The transformation of experience in narrative
    syntax', in Labov, W. *Language in the Inner City*, Philadelphia:
    University of Philadelphia Press
Mayne, Andrew and John Shuttleworth (1986) *Considering Drama*,
    London: Hodder & Stoughton
Ross, Alison (1998) *The Language of Humour*, London: Routledge
Tannen, Deborah (1992) *You Just Don't Understand: Men and Women in
    Conversation*, London: Virago